Strategies for Mobilizing Black Voters

Four Case Studies

Edited by Thomas E. Cavanagh

JCPS

Joint Center for Political Studies
Washington, D.C.
1987

The Joint Center for Political Studies is a national nonprofit institution that conducts research on public policy issues of special concern to black Americans and promotes informed and effective involvement of blacks in the governmental process. Founded in 1970, the Joint Center provides independent and nonpartisan analyses through research, publication, and outreach programs.

Opinions expressed in Joint Center publications are those of the authors and do not necessarily reflect the views of the other staff, officers, or governors of the Joint Center or of the organizations supporting the center and its research.

We gratefully acknowledge the support of the Ford Foundation and The Joyce Foundation, which helped make this publication possible.

Library of Congress Cataloging-in-Publication Data

Strategies for mobilizing Black voters.

   Includes bibliographies.
   1. Afro-Americans—Suffrage—Case studies.
2. Political participation—United States—Case studies. I. Cavanagh, Thomas E. II. Joint Center for Political Studies (U.S.)
JK1924.S92 1987   324.6'23'08996073   87-2668

ISBN 0-941410-48-X

© 1987, Joint Center for Political Studies, Inc.
All Rights Reserved
Printed in the United States of America

1301 Pennsylvania Avenue, N.W.
Suite 400
Washington, D.C. 20004

CONTENTS

	Page
List of Tables	vii
List of Figures	ix
Foreword	xi
About the Authors	xiii
Executive Summary	xvii

1. Understanding Black Voter Turnout: The Strategic Context — 1
Thomas E. Cavanagh

What Makes People Vote?	1
Mobilizing Voters in Four Political Environments	3
Studying Organization, Outreach, and Effectiveness	5
Endnotes	8

2. The Chicago Crusade — 11
Daryl D. Woods

Background	11
Organizational Dynamics	14
Outreach Activities	15
Chicago Black United Communities (CBUC)	15
People Organized for Welfare and Employment Rights (POWER)	18
Voice of the Ethnic Community (VOTE Community)	24
Effectiveness	26
Trends in Voter Registration	27
Trends in Voter Turnout	28
Conclusion	34

cont.

List of Persons Interviewed	35
Endnotes	35

3. Building a Base of Volunteers in Philadelphia   37
Sandra Featherman

Background	38
The Legal Requirements for Registration	38
Previous Elections of Interest to Blacks	41
Opportunity and a Desirable Candidate	43
Organizational Dynamics	44
Registration Efforts	45
Relationships to Outside Groups	47
The Battle of Endorsements	48
Outreach Activities	49
The Goode Campaign	49
The Rizzo Campaign	51
Effectiveness	53
Registration	53
Turnout	55
List of Persons Interviewed	58
Endnotes	59

4. Overcoming the Politics of Polarization in Birmingham   61
Margaret K. Latimer and Robert S. Montjoy

Background	62
The Mayoral Elections of 1979 and 1983	65
The Legal Context	66
Organizational Dynamics	70
Outreach Activities	73
Registration	74
Turnout	75
Effectiveness	79
Registration	80
Turnout	86
Conclusion	90

List of Persons Interviewed	94
Endnotes	95

5. From Pool Hall to Parish House in North Carolina   **101**
Thomas F. Eamon

Background	102
The Michaux Strategy	109
Voter Registration	110
Organizational Dynamics	110
Outreach Activities	112
Effectiveness	116
Voter Turnout	119
Organizational Dynamics	119
Outreach Activities	121
Fund-Raising	123
Effectiveness	125
Conclusion	131
List of Persons Interviewed	133
Endnotes	134

6. Organizing and Educating for Successful Mobilization   **137**
Thomas E. Cavanagh

Organizational Framework	140
Techniques of Educating Voters	143
Endnotes	147

LIST OF TABLES

		Page
2-1.	Special Voter Registration Programs, March 1982 - March 1983 (City of Chicago)	26
2-2.	Registration as a Percentage of Voting-Age Population, 1982-1983 (City of Chicago)	28
2-3.	Voter Turnout as a Percentage of Registration, 1978-1983 (City of Chicago)	29
2-4.	Voter Turnout as a Percentage of Voting-Age Population, 1982-1983 (City of Chicago)	30
3-1.	Growth of Black Voter Registration in Philadelphia, 1975-1983	41
4-1.	Changes in Registration Percentages as a Proportion of Voting-Age Population, by Precinct, 1978-1982 (Jefferson County)	83
4-2.	Differences Between Black and White Registration Percentages as a Proportion of Black and White Voting-Age Populations, Respectively, by Precinct, 1978-1982 (Jefferson County)	85
4-3.	Turnout as a Percentage of Voting-Age Population in Birmingham Precincts, 1978-1982	89
5-1.	Pre-Election Registration, 2nd District (North Carolina), by Race	116
5-2.	Results of First-Round and Run-Off Primaries, 2nd District (North Carolina)	125
5-3.	Turnout in Eastern Counties (2nd District, North Carolina)	129
5-4.	Turnout in Virginia-Border Counties (2nd District, North Carolina)	130

LIST OF FIGURES

		Page
2-1.	Membership Bases of POWER and VOTE Community (City of Chicago)	16
2-2.	Racial Composition of Chicago Wards, 1983	20
2-3.	Wards Won by Candidates in Chicago Mayoral Primary Election, February 22, 1983	32
2-4.	Wards Won by Candidates in Chicago Mayoral General Election, April 12, 1983	33
4-1.	Black Registration as a Percentage of Voting-Age Population, Jefferson County, 1972-1981	81
4-2.	Turnout in Relation to Black Percentage of Population, by Precinct, Jefferson County, 1982 General Election	88
5-1.	North Carolina's 2nd and 4th Congressional Districts Before 1982	103
5-2.	Plan Adopted by State Legislature in 1981 and Rejected by U.S. Department of Justice (2nd and 4th Congressional Districts, North Carolina)	105
5-3.	North Carolina's 2nd and 4th Congressional Districts, 1982 - Present	106

FOREWORD

Black voters have now become a strong, visible force in American politics. This development is reflected in the pivotal role they played in mayoral elections in 1983 in major cities like Chicago, Philadelphia, and Birmingham, where candidates favored by blacks won office. The growing strength of blacks in American politics is also reflected in the decisive role black voters played in several 1986 congressional and senatorial elections. Not only are blacks a steadily increasing proportion of the electorate, but they have also been voting in larger numbers and with greater sophistication than at any time in the country's history.

This study examines one of the major factors contributing to the increase in black political participation: vigorous, creative mobilization efforts. Voter mobilization has always been important in American politics, and especially in recent years it has received considerable emphasis from political parties and candidates. Blacks have been a particularly important target of these efforts because their participation rates have been much lower than those of whites. Despite the importance of voter mobilization, however, we still know relatively little about the various strategies now used to increase voting by blacks or about the effectiveness of those strategies. This publication seeks to shed light on both questions by examining voter mobilization efforts in four widely differing localities: Birmingham, Chicago, Philadelphia, and North Carolina's 2nd Congressional District (Durham).

All four case studies demonstrate remarkably successful mobilization efforts. In the three cities, the efforts also produced victory for the black candidates and substantially increased black political influence. Although circumstances were unique in each jurisdiction, together the cases illustrate strategies and techniques that might be used elsewhere, and underscore the importance of vigorous mobilization drives in any campaign that must rely heavily on black electoral support.

Strategies for Mobilizing Black Voters: Four Case Studies is important, unique, and timely. The Joint Center is proud to make it available to all those—scholars and activists—who are interested in increasing the level and effectiveness of black political participation. We are grateful to the analysts; to Thomas E. Cavanagh, the editor of the volume; to Jane E. Lewin, who prepared the manuscript for publication; and to the other members of the Joint Center staff who helped with production.

Eddie N. Williams

ABOUT THE AUTHORS

THOMAS E. CAVANAGH is a senior research associate with the Committee on the Status of Black Americans of the National Research Council. Before joining the National Research Council he was a senior research associate at the Joint Center for Political Studies. He has also been a guest scholar at the Brookings Institution and has taught at Wesleyan University and Trinity College. A political scientist, he has published widely on black politics, congressional behavior, and voter turnout.

THOMAS F. EAMON is an associate professor of political science at East Carolina University in Greenville, North Carolina, where he teaches courses in southern politics, black politics, and urban policy and administration. He has written numerous articles and papers on black and southern politics and is currently working on a monograph about black community leadership in the South, with an emphasis on Durham. He holds a doctorate in political science from the University of North Carolina at Chapel Hill.

SANDRA FEATHERMAN, an associate professor of political science at Temple University in Philadelphia, is assistant to the president of Temple and acting director of Temple's Center for Public Policy. In addition to writing numerous articles and monographs on local ethnic politics, she has also appeared on more than 100 radio and television news, panel, and talk shows (both national and local) as an analyst of elections and political activities. She holds a doctorate in city and regional planning from the University of Pennsylvania.

MARGARET K. LATIMER is an associate professor of political science at Auburn University in Auburn, Alabama, where she has taught since 1966. She was formerly on the staff of the Institute of Early American History as associate editor of the *William and Mary Quarterly*. She has published numerous articles on American politics, especially on media communication and elections. These include studies of minority representation and mobilization as well as analyses of media use by black voters.

Her research for this volume was supported in part by the Center for Government Services, Auburn University.

ROBERT S. MONTJOY, an associate professor of political science at Auburn University in Auburn, Alabama, is acting head of Auburn's Political Science Department and director of its Master of Public Administration program. He was formerly on the faculty of the University of Virginia. His research interests center on organization theory and public policy. He is the author or co-author of *Regulatory Decision Making* (published by the University Press of Virginia) and articles on policy implementation, public opinion, and job satisfaction.

He has also been active in the field of election administration. He wrote the Alabama *Election Officials' Handbook*; drafted the administrative rules for the use of electronic voting equipment in Alabama; and developed a comprehensive training program for election officials (for which he received the 1982 Public Service award of the Southern Consortium of University Public Service Organizations).

His research for this volume was supported in part by the Center for Government Services, Auburn University.

DARYL D. WOODS is an assistant survey director at the National Opinion Research Center of the University of Chicago. In 1981, while serving as the government relations specialist for the Chicago Urban League, she conducted independent research on the redistricting of Chicago's wards after the 1980 census. Her findings challenged the fairness of the 1981 ward map adopted by the Chicago City Council, and were published in the spring 1982 issue of the Chicago Urban League's *Research Notes* under the title "Redistricting Chicago's Wards: The Question of Racial Equity." She subsequently provided technical assistance and testified as an expert witness at the 1982 federal lawsuit that successfully charged the Chicago City Council with violating provisions of the Voting Rights Act and the U.S. Constitution in its 1981 redistricting.

Ms. Woods, who holds degrees in sociology and city and regional planning, has written articles and reports on urban planning concerns and local political issues.

EXECUTIVE SUMMARY

Civic groups and political organizations continually confront the challenge of how to mobilize the black vote. This study examines some of the means that were used to stimulate black voter participation in four successful voter mobilization drives in 1982 and 1983. The four took place in environments that typify the locations where intensive black political activity is currently taking place:

- two large northern cities (Chicago and Philadelphia): voter outreach and mobilization projects in 1983 succeeded in bringing about the elections of black mayors Harold Washington and Wilson Goode, respectively;
- a majority-black southern city (Birmingham): a black mayor, Richard Arrington, was reelected in 1983 after nearly a decade of black mobilization activity by community groups;
- the small-town and rural South (North Carolina's 2nd Congressional District): in 1982 a black candidate for the Democratic party's nomination for the U.S. House of Representatives, Mickey Michaux, succeeded in greatly increasing the number of blacks registered but lost a run-off primary election.

In each of the four locations, field analysts conducted research on the voter mobilization effort undertaken there. Using a standardized research format, the analysts concentrated on three aspects of the effort in their respective locations:

- organizational dynamics;
- techniques of outreach to the target population; and
- the actual increases in registration and turnout that the total effort produced.

The case studies demonstrate that if organizational efforts are carefully and differentially targeted, enough black voters can be mobilized to mean the difference between success and failure in a given contest. But to actualize the potential of the black vote, groups and candidates must first make blacks aware of their leverage over election outcomes. This awareness is what leads black voters to turn out. To create the awareness and bring the voters out, an organizational framework and techniques of educating voters are necessary.

Organizationally, the four studies imply, a successful voter education effort is difficult to build from scratch; a more promising approach is to build upon a social and political infrastructure already in place. Moreover, it seems to be helpful when the same groups are involved in both the registration and the get-out-the-vote (GOTV) activity; when registration and GOTV are undertaken by different organizations, many newly registered voters may fail to turn out on election day. Other organizational factors that are especially important to the success of a voter education effort are the close supervision and continual monitoring of the progress of registration; support from the local government; and support from local candidates. In terms of how to spend the money that is available, the Chicago experience suggests that a carefully targeted saturation campaign in black media is well worth the expense.

In attempting to educate voters, all four registration campaigns found that flexible registration procedures and ease of registration were important to the success of the effort. And the traditional outreach technique—door-do-door canvassing—appears to be giving way to other techniques: registering people who are gathered together in a group is more efficient than registering people who are approached individually. High-visibility activities reaching out to large numbers of people gathered at a single place appear to register the most people with the least expenditure of effort.

In the four local environments studied, the political loyalties of blacks were sufficiently uniform and predictable that it was usually enough to concentrate on locating unregistered blacks and then to target efforts accordingly, without also worrying about party affiliation. In some of the cases studied, an effort was made to identify and locate more specific subgroups of the black population, such as younger blacks (in Chicago, where that age group traditionally has a low participation rate) or older blacks (in North Carolina, where older people were often reluctant to vote because of the history of intimidation of black voters in the South). It is helpful to associate each target group with an organizational infrastructure, such as schools where the young can be reached or senior citizen centers where the elderly can be.

A voter education campaign needs its messages to be simple and direct. A common thread running through all four campaigns was the idea of removing the act of registering to vote from the context of "politics as usual" and making the candidates and issues appear vitally important to black interests. In other words, the messages could not be abstract appeals to citizenship; they had to be concrete and locally relevant.

Taken as a whole, these case studies show how, with hard work and imagination, a variety of approaches to educating and mobilizing black voters can bear fruit.

1. UNDERSTANDING BLACK VOTER TURNOUT: THE STRATEGIC CONTEXT

Thomas E. Cavanagh

What Makes People Vote?

For many years, black voter turnout in the United States has been considerably lower than white voter turnout. As a result, civic groups and political organizations continually confront the problem of how to mobilize the black vote. This study examines some of the means that were used to stimulate black voter participation in a variety of political environments in the early 1980s.

A successful voter education program makes a person more likely to vote than would be expected, given that person's race, socioeconomic status, and history of political or organizational involvement. The effects of race, status, and involvement are social determinants of voter participation that remain relatively constant over time; these background variables are more or less fixed in advance and must be taken as givens when one is assessing the strategic context for a mobilization effort. In contrast, other determinants of participation are more election-specific and may be more readily manipulated by political strategists in the course of a campaign. The two most important election-specific determinants of participation are intensity of conflict about candidates and issues and personal contact.

Social Determinants of Voter Participation. In general, the more central a role someone plays in the functioning of society, the more likely that person is to vote. Thus, whites, higher-status people, the middle-aged, and non-Southerners are more likely to vote than minorities, lower-status people, the young, and Southerners.[1] Strongly related to these demographic factors are several attitudinal

A successful voter education program makes a person more likely to vote than would be expected, given that person's race, socioeconomic status, and history of political or organizational involvement.

When blacks feel they have a direct stake in the outcome of an election, black turnout can soar dramatically.

traits. Whites, higher-status people, the middle-aged, and non-Southerners are more likely to display—

- interest in electoral campaigns,
- concern about electoral outcomes,
- strong allegiance to a political party,
- belief in the efficacy of political participation, and
- belief that voting is a civic obligation in a democracy.[2]

Each one of these traits increases an individual's likelihood of voting.

The lower socioeconomic status of blacks compared with whites would lead one to expect lower black voter participation on the average, and that is what one finds. But participation has been higher among blacks than among whites of similar status, apparently because a countervailing attitudinal trait neutralizes the effects of social status: a sense of racial solidarity, generated by experiences of oppression, has heightened blacks' interest in voting.[3]

Membership in voluntary associations, community groups, and churches is also associated with higher turnout. Here the effect is probably indirect: such memberships essentially express a sense of social cohesiveness, but they link the individual to a communications network that facilitates electoral mobilization.[4]

Election-Specific Determinants of Voter Participation. Of the two principal election-specific determinants of turnout, the more important is intensity of conflict about individual candidates or issues. Voter participation usually rises if the electorate perceives clear and significant differences between the two choices. An election presenting starkly defined alternatives that reflect emotionally charged community conflicts can stimulate a large increase in turnout, particularly among lower-status voters. When blacks feel they have a direct stake in the outcome of an election, black turnout can soar dramatically. Between 1967 and 1983 this pattern was strikingly evidenced by the massive mobilization of black voters to elect black mayors in Atlanta, Chicago,

Cleveland, Gary, Los Angeles, Newark, and Philadelphia.[5] Similarly, in the 1964 presidential election large numbers of blacks went to the polls to register their approval of President Lyndon Johnson for advocating the Civil Rights Act and the Great Society, and their opposition to Senator Barry Goldwater. In the 1984 presidential election black turnout was also high, this time in opposition to the policies of President Ronald Reagan.[6]

Whatever the intensity of the conflicts expressed in an election campaign, contact by party or campaign workers can stimulate turnout. The more personal the contact (e.g., personal visits or telephone calls, as opposed to mailings), the more pronounced the effect. Thus, when traditional party organizations or grassroots efforts on behalf of individual candidates use interpersonal networking, they can raise the level of black voter turnout.[7]

Mobilizing Voters in Four Political Environments

To examine some of the strategies that have been used to increase black voter participation, the Joint Center for Political Studies commissioned research on four voter mobilization projects conducted in 1982 and 1983. The purpose of the research was to isolate factors associated with the successful mobilization of the black electorate. The projects analyzed were—

- the voter outreach project undertaken in Chicago between July 1982 and April 1983 in preparation for Harold Washington's ultimately successful mayoral campaign;
- the voter registration drive undertaken in Philadelphia in 1983 in preparation for Wilson Goode's ultimately successful mayoral campaign;
- the decade-long black mobilization campaign of community groups in Birmingham, Alabama, culminating in the reelection victory of Mayor Richard Arrington in 1983; and
- the voter registration drive conducted in 1982 by H. M. "Mickey" Michaux in his ultimately

Contact by party or campaign workers can stimulate turnout.

unsuccessful bid for the Democratic nomination for Congress in North Carolina's largely rural 2nd Congressional District.

These four voter mobilization efforts were chosen not only because they were important, interesting, and successful in dramatically increasing black voter registration and turnout, but also because their locations typify the variety of environments in which intensive black political activity is currently taking place. Two of the sites, Chicago and Philadelphia, are large northern cities; one, Birmingham, is a majority-black southern city (population nearly 300,000); and one, the 2nd Congressional District in North Carolina, exemplifies conditions in the small-city and rural South.

Harold Washington's mayoral campaign in Chicago is perhaps the most outstanding example in modern times of successful voter mobilization activity at the grassroots level. For years, city hall and the Daley-era Cook County Democratic machine had been unresponsive to black interests. By the late 1970s, South Side blacks were regularly supporting insurgent candidates over those backed by the machine for ward-level offices. Then a series of politically alienating decisions by Mayor Jane Byrne in 1981 and 1982 catalyzed community efforts to draft a black mayoral candidate and to register enough voters to elect him.

Like Chicago, Philadelphia is a northern industrial city with a 40 percent black population that had long been a junior partner in an entrenched political machine dominated by conservative white ethnics. But in two ways, developments in Philadelphia in the early 1980s differed strikingly from those in Chicago. In Chicago, blacks openly revolted against the local Democratic machine (and have remained apart from it: under the leadership of party chairman Ed Vrdolyak, a bloc of white ethnics on the city council has continued to oppose black aspirations for power, even with Harold Washington as mayor). In Philadelphia, in contrast, Wilson Goode successfully sought to control the Democratic machine from within by endorsing and carrying to victory with him a slate of city council candidates. And whereas registration efforts in Chicago were conducted al-

*I*n two ways, developments in Philadelphia in the early 1980s differed strikingly from those in Chicago.

most entirely by nonpartisan groups, in Philadelphia much of the registration activity was coordinated by Goode's campaign workers.

Birmingham illustrates the political progress made by blacks in the South since passage of the Voting Rights Act in 1965. This former bastion of white supremacy elected a black mayor, Richard Arrington, in 1979. Once Arrington was elected, he secured his political base by encouraging flexible voter registration procedures—a flexibility that, in Chicago, was achieved only after a prolonged court battle. In Birmingham as in Chicago, however, the involvement of community-based organizations in voter registration and get-out-the-vote efforts was significant.

Birmingham illustrates the political progress made by blacks in the South since passage of the Voting Rights Act in 1965.

The North Carolina case study offers a rather different perspective on black voter mobilization. The largely rural character of Michaux's congressional district made grassroots organizing more labor-intensive than it might have been in a more geographically compact urban setting. And because a federal office was at stake, labor unions and national lobbies played a more active role than they did in the mayoral campaigns. Most importantly, however, Michaux's campaign is interesting as an example of the difficulties that run-off primaries often create for black candidates. Michaux led in the first primary, but in the run-off most of the whites who had voted for the third-place finisher shifted their support to the white candidate who had been the second-place finisher, costing Michaux the nomination. Jesse Jackson often cited the Michaux experience when speaking out against run-off primaries in his 1984 presidential campaign.

Studying Organization, Outreach, and Effectiveness

In each of the four locations, one or more analysts conducted research on the voter mobilization efforts. The analysts' primary sources of information were interviews with people involved in the local

Michaux's campaign [in North Carolina] is interesting as an example of the difficulties that run-off primaries often create for black candidates.

voter education effort,* organizational records (where available), press clippings, and local registration and voting data. Although the field investigators were free to explore idiosyncratic local circumstances, they adhered to a standardized research format to ensure that certain topics were covered in each case study, so as to facilitate comparisons.

The analysts concentrated on three aspects of the voter education effort in their respective locations:

- organizational dynamics;
- techniques of outreach to the target population; and
- effectiveness of the total effort.

Organizational Dynamics. In studying organizational dynamics, the analysts first had to identify the groups involved in the voter education effort. Then, because black voter mobilization is invariably a coalition activity, they examined the apportioning of organizational tasks and goals among the various elements of each local coalition. Previous research and abundant anecdotal evidence had suggested that two types of distinctions would be particularly important:

- the distinction between partisan and nonpartisan activity; and
- the distinction between, on the one hand, voter registration and education activity and, on the other hand, election day get-out-the-vote (GOTV) activity; that distinction is important because the two activities are often conducted by different groups.

Other factors relevant to organizational dynamics were—

- the attitudes of local government officials and candidates toward the registration and get-out-the-vote activity;
- the raising and spending of money; and
- each group's previous involvement in black registration efforts.

---

*A list of the people interviewed appears at the end of each chapter.

Outreach Activities. In analyzing the techniques employed to mobilize the black community, we bore in mind that voter education efforts inevitably face tradeoffs in allocating the scarce resources of money and volunteer time. Thus, we wished to determine which types of outreach—whether door-to-door canvassing, the use of leaflets, or media advertising—were considered most efficient and effective. We were especially interested in the matter of "on-site" registration: allowing deputy registrars to register people at shopping centers, public libraries, unemployment offices, and other community locations, as opposed to requiring that registration be conducted only in traditional registration offices.

Whatever type of outreach is used, the most critical task facing any voter education effort is probably that of identifying, locating, and then conveying messages to the target population of nonvoters. This task requires, first, that registration statistics be matched with demographic characteristics in given geographic areas. Areas characterized by low registration and a high share of the demographically defined target population then become the focus of activity. And in selecting themes and slogans to mobilize those habitual nonvoters, one must make assumptions about their motivations. Our field investigators, therefore, examined the types of messages employed and the particular choice of communications media (black radio, direct mail, etc.) for conveying them.

Effectiveness. Our final objective was to measure the effectiveness of each program. Political activists have a stake in claiming credit for increasing the turnout among targeted constituent groups; thus, before considering a group's claims to be valid, a researcher must corroborate those claims with evidence from official voting statistics. The field investigators therefore compared registration and turnout figures for black and white areas before and after the voter mobilization drive in question.

The most critical task facing any voter education effort is probably that of identifying, locating, and then conveying messages to the target population of nonvoters.

Chapters 2-5 of this volume present the findings of the four sets of field investigators. Chapter 6 is a summary and conclusion prepared by the editor. It is our hope that both scholars and practitioners will find this collection a useful addition to the literature on American voter participation.

Endnotes

1. Much of this discussion is taken from Thomas E. Cavanagh, *Black Voter Participation in the United States: A Review of the Literature* (Washington, D.C.: Joint Center for Political Studies, 1983). The definitive treatment of the demographic determinants of American voter turnout is Raymond E. Wolfinger and Steven J. Rosenstone, *Who Votes?* (New Haven: Yale University Press, 1980). An extensive discussion of the literature appears in Lester W. Milbrath and M. L. Goel, *Political Participation,* 2nd ed. (Chicago: Rand McNally, 1977).

2. Angus Campbell, Philip E. Converse, Warren E. Miller, and Donald E. Stokes, *The American Voter* (New York: John Wiley, 1960), chapter 5.

3. Richard D. Shingles, "Black Consciousness and Political Participation: The Missing Link," *American Political Science Review,* 75 (March 1981), 76-91.

4. Sidney Verba and Norman H. Nie, *Participation in America* (New York: Harper and Row, 1972).

5. The literature on black mayoral campaigns is reviewed in Thomas E. Cavanagh and Denise Stockton, *Black Elected Officials and Their Constituencies* (Washington, D.C.: Joint Center for Political Studies, 1983), and Thomas F. Pettigrew, "Black Mayoral Campaigns," in *Urban Governance and Minorities,* ed. Herrington J. Bryce (New York: Praeger, 1976). For a comprehensive analysis of black voter mobilization activity in the 1967 campaigns of Carl Stokes in Cleveland, Ohio, and Richard Hatcher in Gary, Indiana, see William E. Nelson and Philip J. Meranto, *Electing Black May-*

ors: Political Action in the Black Community (Columbus, Ohio: Ohio State University Press, 1977).

6. Thomas E. Cavanagh, *Inside Black America* (Washington, D.C.: Joint Center for Political Studies, 1985).

7. Bernard R. Berelson, Paul F. Lazarsfeld, and William N. McPhee, *Voting* (Chicago: University of Chicago Press, 1954); Paul Carton, *Mobilizing the Black Community: The Effects of Personal Contact Campaigning on Black Voters* (Washington, D.C.: Joint Center for Political Studies, 1984); Samuel J. Eldersveld, "Experimental Propaganda Techniques and Voting Behavior," *American Political Science Review*, 50 (March 1956), 154-165; Penn Kimball, *The Disconnected* (New York: Columbia University Press, 1972).

2. THE CHICAGO CRUSADE
Daryl D. Woods

In 1983 Harold Washington became the first black mayor in Chicago's history. His election was brought about mainly by an intensive voter registration drive within the city's black community. Over a 12-month period beginning in March 1982, more than 150,000 people, mostly in black wards, registered to vote. That massive, unprecedented increase in registrants had a bearing on three major elections:

- the November 1982 gubernatorial election (between incumbent Republican James Thompson and Democrat Adlai Stevenson III);
- the February 1983 Democratic mayoral primary (among incumbent Jane Byrne and challengers Richard M. Daley and Harold Washington); and
- the April 1983 general mayoral election (between Republican Bernard Epton and Democrat Harold Washington).

Background

In 1982 and 1983, voter registration in Chicago spread like "a fever within the black community" (in the words of political activist and radio commentator Lu Palmer). A combination of factors was responsible, including an increase in the proportion of the city's population that was black, dissatisfaction with Mayor Byrne's policies, and a stepped-up effort by local black leaders to inform blacks about the issues and about the importance of political involvement.

On the basis of population, blacks certainly had the potential to become a decisive force in local and state elections. According to 1980 census figures, they constituted 40 percent of the city's total population and 36 percent of its voting-age population. But low registration and turnout rates in comparison

In 1982 and 1983, voter registration in Chicago spread like "a fever within the black community."

with the rates for whites were the chief reason for the relatively low political effectiveness of blacks.

Dissatisfaction with the policies of the mayor (and with the actions of selected public officials generally) was widespread among blacks. Many community leaders had long felt that Chicago's white leadership had traditionally failed to address minority concerns adequately.

In an effort to heighten black awareness and electoral participation, numerous organizations worked together in initiating a voter registration drive. The drive began as a public dialogue on community issues among organizations with varying degrees of political involvement. The thread linking their activities was the belief that a black could be elected mayor if blacks voted in record numbers and if the white and Hispanic communities gave the candidate some measure of support.

In their campaign to persuade blacks to vote, the organizations decided to focus upon concrete, achievable objectives, as recommended by previous analyses of black voter mobilization in Chicago. A 1981 study by the Chicago Urban League, for example, had concluded that (a) the reason many blacks failed to participate in the electoral process was that they lacked rudimentary information about local and national political figures and issues, and (b) attempts to convince those people of the general importance of voting might not prove effective. Instead, "ongoing efforts to inform the public about key public officials and specific volatile issues are essential if registering and voting are to become frequent and meaningful acts."[1] Because of their immediate impact upon minorities, the policies of the Republican administration in Washington and of Republican Governor James Thompson (during the first phase) and of Democratic Mayor Jane Byrne (during the later phases) became the focus of voter registration activities.

Republican Governor Thompson had long been under fire from community leaders and local residents for his administration's indifferent performance on social welfare issues and other minority concerns, but Democrat Byrne was a different mat-

In an effort to heighten black awareness and electoral participation, numerous organizations worked together in initiating a voter registration drive.

ter. Blacks had traditional loyalties to the local Democratic party. Her 1979 election campaign—capped by the theme of "One Chicago"—had contributed to raising social, economic, and political expectations among black voters, and a majority of them had supported her candidacy. But when Byrne failed to fulfill those expectations and, in fact, made a series of controversial appointments and supported a number of controversial programs, the black community turned its back on her, too.

The actions of the Chicago City Council and Mayor Byrne that jolted the black population and captured immediate media attention were the following:

- On April 22, 1981, two opponents of federally imposed desegregation (Betty Bonow and Rose Mary Janus) were appointed to the Chicago Board of Education. Their appointments reduced the number of blacks on the 11-member board to 3, even though the pupil population of the school system was approximately 61 percent black.
- On November 30, 1981, the City Council adopted a ward redistricting map that lessened the electoral chances of black and Hispanic candidates. (In 1982, the U.S. Department of Justice successfully filed suit against the city to gain additional wards where blacks or Hispanics were the majority.)
- On July 23, 1982, three whites (Angeline Caruso, Estelle Holzer, and Andrew Mooney) were appointed to the Chicago Housing Authority (CHA) Board. Their appointments reduced the number of blacks on the 10-member board to 3, even though the tenant population in public housing administered by the CHA was 85 percent black.

Shortly after the appointment of the three whites to the Chicago Housing Authority Board, a caller on a black radio program (Derek Hill's "Sunday Morning Live" on WBMX-FM) suggested that blacks protest the appointment by boycotting the city-sponsored Chicago Fest. Chicago Fest, an annual summer lakefront event featuring ethnic foods and

In their campaign to persuade blacks to vote, the organizations decided to focus upon concrete, achievable objectives.

If . . . three conditions were met, the crusade to mobilize the black vote on behalf of a black candidate would have a chance of succeeding.

musical entertainment, was one of Jane Byrne's pet projects. Jesse Jackson, who was a guest on the radio program, thought the idea of the boycott was tremendous, as did other black leaders.

Although promoters of Chicago Fest tried to minimize the impact of the boycott, profits dropped from $1,064,360 in 1981 to $440,206 in 1982.[2] Beyond that, the boycott was a vital psychological and organizational means of increasing black political awareness and involvement. It helped establish a climate conducive to voter registration and electoral participation.

Several months later, Dr. Roger Fox of the Chicago Urban League projected outcomes for the Democratic mayoral primary under varying assumptions. His model showed that the odds for a black candidate improved if a minimum of two white candidates split the white vote. Approximately 625,000 blacks, or 80 percent of the black voting-age population, would have to be registered. The model assumed a voter turnout of 70 percent of the registration level for the black and white populations; the black candidate would have to receive at least 80 percent of the black vote and 10 percent of the white vote.

Thus, a black mayoral candidacy could become a viable political option under these conditions:

- a registration rate of 80 percent or greater among voting-age blacks;
- the presence of at least two white candidates in the Democratic primary who would split the white vote; and
- cohesiveness of the black vote.

If all three conditions were met, the crusade to mobilize the black vote on behalf of a black candidate would have a chance of succeeding.

Organizational Dynamics

The principal vehicles established by community-based groups for nonpartisan outreach registration[3] in 1982 and 1983 were two umbrella organizations, POWER (People Organized for Welfare and Employment Rights) and VOTE Community (Voice of the Ethnic Community). Participants in one or both of the coalitions included PUSH, the Chicago Urban League, Heart of Uptown Coalition, the People's Movement for Voter Registration, and the Illinois Welfare Rights Organization. Most had worked together in the past, either on voter education projects or on community issues. Both POWER and VOTE Community began separate but cooperative programs during the summer of 1982.

A third coalition, CBUC (Chicago Black United Communities, pronounced "C-Buck"), could not participate directly in outreach registration because of past partisan political work. However, CBUC played a major role in promoting black electoral participation and laying the groundwork for a black mayoral candidacy.

Together, POWER, VOTE Community, and CBUC were central in the events leading to Harold Washington's election victory. Each coalition developed a specific strategy for maximizing black electoral participation. POWER initiated two lawsuits to gain access to welfare and unemployment offices for use as outreach registration sites. VOTE Community, to motivate both registration and turnout, created a sophisticated media campaign to complement the various grassroots programs. (Figure 2-1 is a diagram of the membership bases of POWER and VOTE Community.) CBUC held rallies, demonstrations, and political education classes to increase black awareness of the ways in which local political institutions (like the Democratic party, the Chicago City Council, and the mayor's office) operate.

Each coalition [POWER, VOTE Community, and CBUC] developed a specific strategy for maximizing black electoral participation.

Outreach Activities

Chicago Black United Communities (CBUC)

The first of the three coalitions to be formed was CBUC. Radio commentator and activist Lu Palmer founded it in March 1980 in response to a specific

Figure 2-1
Membership Bases of POWER and VOTE Community (City of Chicago)

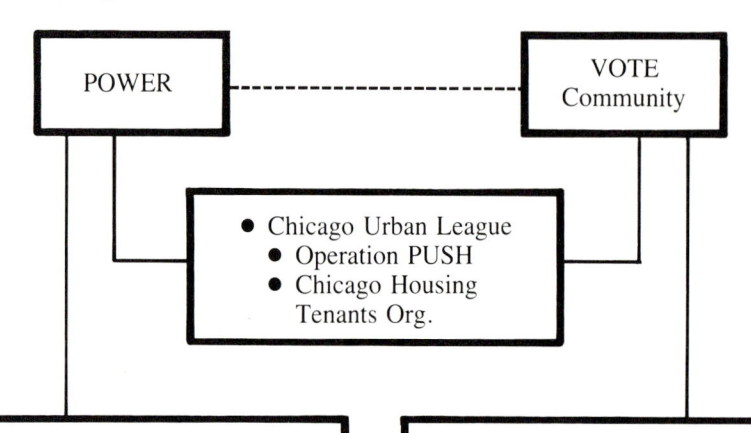

```
    ┌─────────┐                    ┌─────────────┐
    │  POWER  │--------------------│    VOTE     │
    │         │                    │  Community  │
    └─────────┘                    └─────────────┘
```

- Chicago Urban League
- Operation PUSH
- Chicago Housing Tenants Org.

POWER:

Midwest Community Council
Heart of Uptown Coalition
The Public Welfare Coalition
The All People's Congress
The Chicago Area Black Lung Association
The Chicago Gray Panthers
The Southeast Welfare Concerned Recipient Org.
The South Austin Community Coalition
The Kenwood-Oakland Community Org.
The Tranquility-Marksman Memorial Org.
The Chicago Welfare Rights Org.
The Westtown Concerned Citizens Coalition
The Pilsen Housing and Business Alliance
The Parent Equalizers of Chicago
The Mid-Austin Steering Committee
Westside People for Progress
W.H.I.P.P. (Working Hard in the Interest of People Protection)
Concerned Young Adults

VOTE Community:

Soft Sheen Products, Inc.
The Afro-American Police League
The Black Illinois Legislative Lobby
Ethnic Communications Outlet
Voter Registration Task Force
Peoples Action Coalition (PACI)
The Peoples Movement for Voter Registration
The Woodlawn Org.
Leon's Bar-B-Que
Salter & Cater Advertising
Chicago Area Alliance of Black School Educators

grievance against Mayor Byrne's administration: Palmer and other community activists felt that community participation in the selection of nominees to the Chicago Board of Education had been inadequate, although 5 of the 11 positions were filled by blacks. Palmer contended that Byrne had solicited input chiefly from the Chicago Urban League and Chicago United, a consortium of black, white, and Hispanic business executives.

In addition to founding CBUC, Palmer was an early promoter of the idea that a black mayoral campaign would be viable in 1983. He began acting on that belief on August 15, 1981, when CBUC held a political education conference that had two goals: to retire some aldermen who represented black wards but had not been responsive to CBUC's constituents, and to elect a black mayor in 1983.

"We considered that conference to be the launching pad for the drive for a black mayor," Palmer said. "What we did at CBUC was set out to develop a mindset among blacks. By that we mean, to get it on their minds that we could elect a black mayor and, indeed, that we would."

The hallmark of CBUC's campaign was the slogan "We Shall See in '83." Palmer coined it, and through CBUC's literature and Palmer's radio programs, "Lu's Notebook" and "On Target," it firmly implanted itself in the minds of many black people.[4]

After the 1981 conference, CBUC organized a political education effort in the form of a series of four-week clinics for people interested in developing and operating political campaigns. Next, in July 1982, Palmer conducted a black mayoral survey, using small community newspapers and the major, black-owned *Chicago Defender* to determine candidate preference among the black population. A month later he followed up the survey with a mayoral plebiscite at Bethel AME Church, where the general public voted on the top 10 choices identified in the survey. In both the survey and the plebiscite, Congressman Harold Washington was the favored candidate—the choice of 78 percent of the respondents in the survey and 91 percent in the plebiscite.

CBUC organized a political education effort in the form of a series of four-week clinics for people interested in developing and operating political campaigns.

> *[Harold] Washington said he would not consider running unless 50,000 additional people registered to vote by the November elections.*

At the time of the plebiscite, Washington said he would not consider running unless 50,000 additional people registered to vote by the November elections. CBUC was instrumental in organizing the People's Movement for Voter Registration (a coalition of individuals and organizations that eventually became part of VOTE Community). But after the Chicago Board of Elections determined that CBUC had been partisan in its support of 17th Ward Alderman Allan Streeter in his June 1982 election bid against Byrne-backed candidate Jewel Frierson, CBUC had to relinquish its role in the People's Movement and was barred from participating in outreach voter registration.

Throughout 1981 and 1982, Palmer's radio commentary and confrontations with the Byrne administration, together with the programs of other community activists and local politicians, were creating a promising climate for a black candidacy. He increased the visibility and volatility of local political issues. During the period of Byrne's most controversial actions, for example, he garnered considerable attention from the media, and particularly from black radio stations and the *Chicago Defender*. On one memorable occasion, when he led a demonstration at the Chicago Housing Authority offices to protest the appointment of the three whites to the board of directors, his action received page-one press coverage and appeared on local evening television news broadcasts. When commenting later on the success of the voter drive, he said, "Mayor Byrne with her insults was really helping us because whenever she did something that was a slap in the face we would just say, 'You see why we need a black mayor.'"

People Organized for Welfare and Employment Rights (POWER)

A large measure of the success of the 1982-1983 voter registration drive was attributable to the savvy of leaders like Walter "Slim" Coleman, a veteran community organizer and president of the Heart of Uptown Coalition on the city's North Side. Heart of Uptown provides community services to a white, Hispanic, and black constituent base.

Coleman helped form POWER, a coalition of 21 civil rights, welfare rights, and community groups organized around welfare and unemployment issues, in December 1981, and he served as the group's vice president. He described POWER as "a coalition of groups that have worked together on different issues [at different times] . . . over the past 15 years." Each group had its own level of involvement in city issues. Many (like PUSH, the Chicago Urban League, and Heart of Uptown) had conducted voter registration drives during the preceding 8-10 years.

The welfare and unemployment issues that were behind the founding of POWER became especially prominent between August 1981 and July 1982. Despite marches, demonstrations, and lobbying, the U.S. Congress, the Illinois legislature, and the Chicago City Council all enacted cutbacks in social programs for the state's and the city's poor:

- In August 1981, Congress reduced food stamp, housing, and AFDC benefits (Omnibus Budget Reconciliation Act, PL 97-35).
- Between September 1981 and July 1982, Governor Thompson reduced general assistance payments and the grant paid to the aged and disabled, and tightened Medicaid eligibility rules for children and the aged and disabled.
- In March 1982, the Chicago City Council and Mayor Byrne failed to fund emergency shelters, and reduced funding for food pantries.

Along with other POWER participants, Coleman felt that

> the position of people who were unemployed and on public aid wasn't well represented or well respected at the spring 1982 session of the state legislature. We decided to move on a voter registration drive that would register a significant force that could then be used to influence the legislators. The best places to register that constituency were unemployment and public aid offices.

Consequently, in July 1982 POWER's organizers began a series of negotiations at 35 sites. (Figure 2-2 is a map of Chicago's wards by racial composi-

Throughout 1981 and 1982, . . . the programs of . . . community activists and local politicians were creating a promising climate for a black candidacy.

THE CHICAGO CRUSADE

Figure 2-2
Racial Composition of Chicago Wards, 1983

LEGEND

☐ Wards 50% or more white

▤ Wards 50% or more Hispanic

▦ Wards 50% or more black

▨ Mixed wards—less than 50% of any racial group

• Public aid / unemployment offices— POWER voter registration program

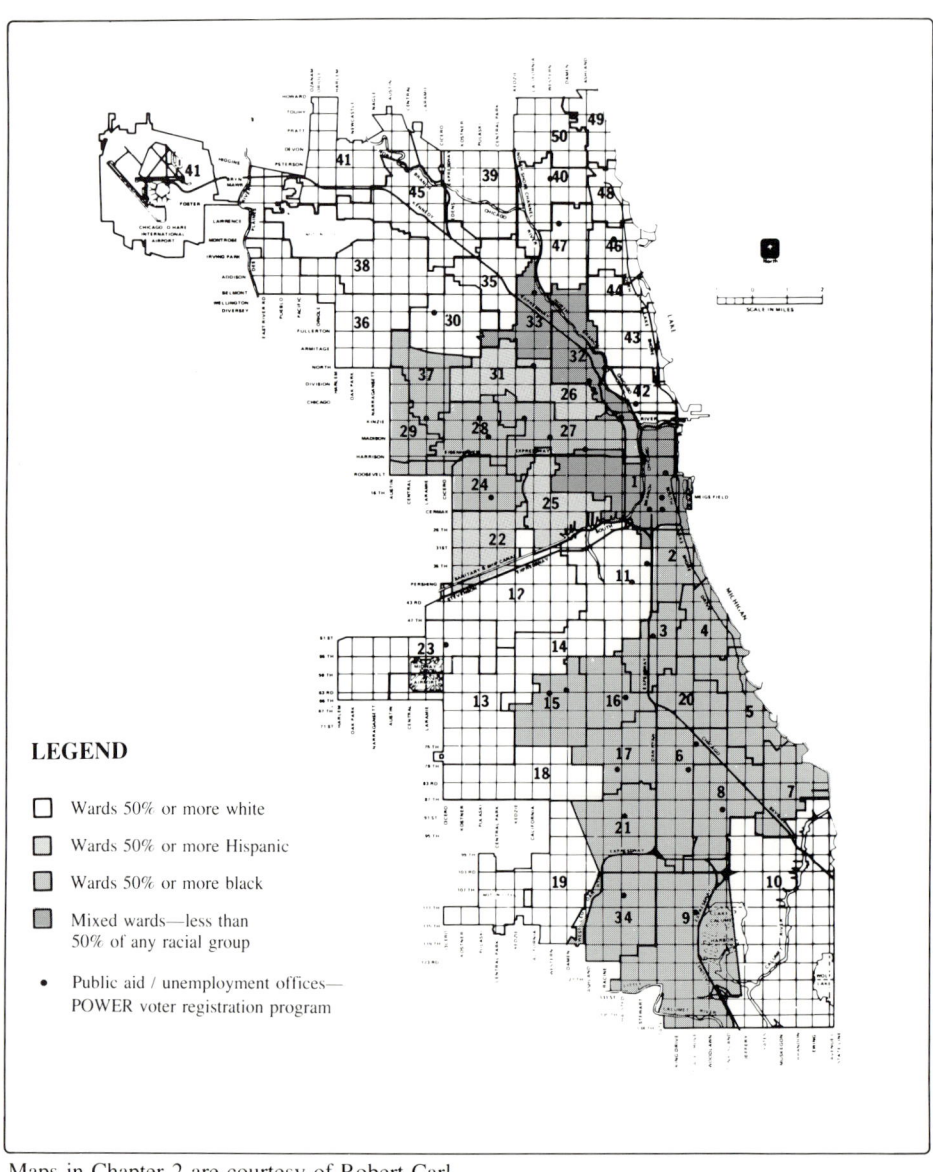

Maps in Chapter 2 are courtesy of Robert Carl.

tion, with the location of the public aid and unemployment offices covered under POWER's program.)

The Chicago Board of Elections had complete discretion over the operation of voter registration programs. In 1982, citizens could register either at the downtown Board of Elections office during normal business hours or, under a program in existence since 1973, at special outreach sites in local communities. The special sites—generally public libraries, public schools, and churches—were operated on a limited or temporary basis, sometimes only upon request by nonpartisan community groups.

All outreach sites had to be manned by Board of Elections employees, and only Board of Elections employees were qualified to serve as registrars. Moreover, staff availability for specific projects was subject to board approval. In the opinion of attorney Thomas Johnson of the Legal Assistance Foundation of Chicago, this requirement "created an incredible obstacle" to community-based organizations.

The Legal Assistance Foundation of Chicago represented POWER in negotiations and litigation to establish temporary registration programs at 35 offices of the Illinois Department of Public Aid and the Illinois Department of Labor during August and September 1982 (before the gubernatorial election).[5] State officials had prohibited voter registration inside the waiting rooms of both departments (POWER v. Thompson, Case No. 82-C-5024), maintaining that voter registration might "(a) disrupt business at the offices; or (b) lead applicants and recipients to believe that registration was a condition to receiving benefits."[6] On August 16, 1982, POWER filed a federal lawsuit against Governor Thompson, the directors of the two departments, and the Board of Elections, seeking to conduct voter registration in public offices. On August 19, 1982, the lawsuit was settled. POWER volunteers were given access to waiting rooms to speak with clients, but registration had to be conducted outside using unmarked vans and card tables provided by POWER.

> *"The best places to register [people who were unemployed and on public aid] were unemployment and public aid offices."*

POWER filed a federal lawsuit . . . seeking to conduct voter registration in public offices.

POWER's first drive took place on the 7 working days between August 12 and August 20, 1982, and the 20 working days between August 30 and September 27, 1982. Negotiations and litigation with state officials and the Chicago Board of Elections effectively prevented POWER from following up on its original proposal for the first drive, which was to conduct registration on every working day between August 1, 1982, and September 30, 1982.

During POWER's first drive, more than 42,000 new low-income voters were registered. It was the most successful special registration effort in the city's history, according to a Board of Elections announcement.[7]

On November 22, 1982, POWER filed another lawsuit to obtain the right to conduct a second registration drive, this one before the 1983 mayoral primary and general elections (POWER v. Thompson, Case No. 82-C-7144). State officials had again refused to permit registration inside the offices of the Department of Public Aid and the Department of Labor, even though the drive would be conducted in the winter months. On December 3, at the pre-trial conference, the Board of Elections agreed to provide registrars at state offices if POWER would agree to (1) reduce the length of the project from 751 site-days to 231 site-days, and (2) execute the drive in a manner consistent with the Board of Elections concept of nonpartisanship. (Slim Coleman did not participate in the second drive because of his open support for Washington.)

On December 10, 1982, the District Court entered a temporary restraining order against the defendants, and on January 17, 1983, POWER completed the drive. Approximately 9,000 persons were registered, according to attorney Johnson. Later in January, POWER voluntarily moved to dismiss its case. The presiding judge awarded attorneys' fees to the Legal Assistance Foundation of Chicago, to be paid by state officials and not the Board of Elections.

Slim Coleman estimates that the total cost of the POWER registration effort, excluding attorneys' fees paid by the state defendants, was about $20,000. This money was used to rent vans to serve as mobile registration units. The Chicago Board of Elections had only two vans, which were not sufficient to cover the 35 registration sites at the offices of the Department of Public Aid and the Department of Labor. Since the drive was nonpartisan, funds for van rentals for the first drive—during the period before the November 2 gubernatorial election—were solicited by mail from Democratic and Republican party officials and a variety of other sources. Contributors included Democratic gubernatorial candidate Adlai Stevenson III ($10,000), the Illinois State Central Democratic Committee ($3,000), the Richard M. Daley Campaign Committee ($1,000), and the American Federation of State, County, and Municipal Employees ($5,000). Money was not needed for vans for the second registration drive, the one leading to the mayoral primary, because that drive was conducted inside state offices.

Each organization in POWER was responsible for supplying volunteers to specific registration sites, with the work load divided on a geographical basis. Coleman noted that some communications problems existed—any project with 21 organizations involved in a coordinated effort is likely to have internal problems—but those problems were inconsequential in comparison with the difficulties of negotiating with the Board of Elections and state officials and raising money for vans.

In Coleman's opinion, the outreach effort was successful because it was aimed at a particular segment of the population (people on public aid and unemployment) and because project volunteers came from the same economic and social class as the people they were trying to register. Success may also have been due to the implicit message, which was that people on public aid and unemployment had as much right to register to vote, and as much of a duty to do so, as anyone else.

Dr. Lawrence Saunders of the Chicago Urban League attributed the success of the voter drive to "system penetration"; that is, the voter registration drive focused on those governmental offices where the greatest number of potential new voters was to be found.

POWER's first drive ... was the most successful special registration effort in the city's history.

Voice of the Ethnic Community (VOTE Community)

VOTE Community (Voice of the Ethnic Community) was the umbrella organization for a variety of groups and individuals engaged in motivating people to register and vote.[8] Its members included the Afro-American Police League, the Chicago Urban League, the People's Movement for Voter Registration, the Woodlawn Organization, PUSH, and Soft Sheen Products, Inc.

The genesis of VOTE Community was a meeting between Renault Robinson (former executive director of the Afro-American Police League and the campaign manager for Harold Washington in the 1977 mayoral election) and Edward Gardner (president of Soft Sheen Products, Inc., a Chicago-based, black-owned, hair-care-products concern).[9] Robinson asked Gardner's help in developing promotion for a massive voter registration campaign for Chicago's black electorate. The result was VOTE Community, a partnership of citizens, community organizations, and businesses that was formed in the summer of 1982, shortly after POWER began its outreach registration activities.

VOTE Community's goal was the registration of 100,000 new voters by October 5, 1982, which was Precinct Registration Day, the last date for registration before the November 2 gubernatorial election. For this traditional special one-day registration period, the Board of Elections provides 3,000 additional registration sites at local polling places throughout the city.

Member organizations and individuals working on their own focused on outreach registration at the grassroots level, including programs at churches, parades, and local events. Outreach registration programs were targeted at the black wards that had the greatest discrepancy between the number of registrants and the voting-age population. Registration statistics by ward were obtained from the Chicago Board of Elections, and the voting-age population by race was calculated from census data.

Soft Sheen Products provided financial resources and legal, marketing, and advertising expertise for

The outreach effort was successful because it was aimed at a particular segment of the population . . . and because project volunteers came from the same economic and social class as the people they were trying to register.

developing a media campaign to support the VOTE Community registration and education program. The company contributed $150,000 of the $200,000 spent on the media campaign, and Emma Young, the company's creative director, developed it. Radio commercials featuring rap, music, and personalities were aired on all the major black radio stations, and posters, banners, and bumper stickers were distributed throughout the city. The predominantly black and Hispanic wards, particularly areas with comparatively high levels of unregistered voters, were saturated with printed material. After the campaign, the general consensus among Soft Sheen staff was that radio had proved most effective in reaching VOTE Community's target group.

In Young's words, "We had one theme: 'Come Alive, October Five—Register to Vote.'" That theme was used in all the promotional material. Young said that Soft Sheen chose "Come Alive, October Five" because the company wanted to focus on the date and not on an idea or even on the concept "register to vote." Neither did the company want to give people a reason for registering or voting. "We wanted to focus on a date so the theme would be a call to action. People would have something to do at a particular time and in a particular place, which is the polling place nearest their home."

Soft Sheen narrowed its market, or target population, to blacks between the ages of 18 and 34. Young black people generally do not register and vote in the same proportion as older blacks. Emma Young believed this age differential was attributable to a sense of hopelessness rather than apathy. On a political and social level, she felt that "young Chicagoans really didn't have any options. They really didn't have any choices."

Later, in the 1983 registration drives leading to the mayoral primary and general elections, VOTE Community again used the same basic strategy. January 25 and March 14, respectively, were the precinct registration dates, and "Keep It Alive" messages replaced "Come Alive, October Five," as part of a program to reach persons who had not yet registered.

VOTE Community's goal was the registration of 100,000 new voters by . . . the last date for registration before the . . . gubernatorial election.

Effectiveness

The 12 months preceding the 1983 mayoral election represented a landmark in the 10-year history of Chicago's Special Voter Registration Programs. More than 150,000 people were registered, or almost 40 percent of the total 379,541 outreach registrations recorded in the entire decade from March 1973 to March 1983. A breakdown of the total registrations between 1982 and 1983 by site is presented in Table 2-1.[10]

The general consensus ... was that radio had proved most effective in reaching VOTE Community's target group.

Table 2-1
Special Voter Registration Programs, March 1982 - March 1983 (City of Chicago)

Program	Number Registered*
Special registration activities sponsored by community groups (sites included churches, banks, and shopping centers)	21,983
Public aid and unemployment offices (POWER program)	48,844
Library voter registration program	76,790
High school/college registration program	2,570
New citizens' receptions	1,806
Total	151,993

*The figures cited in this table are the official final registration counts reported by the Chicago Board of Elections after canvassing eligible voters.

For CBUC, POWER, and VOTE Community organizers, Harold Washington's election as mayor was proof enough of the success of their activities. POWER and VOTE Community did not conduct internal evaluations of any aspect of their voter drives, although they did keep unofficial records on the number of registrations per unemployment and public aid site. Both coalitions targeted blacks, Hispanics, and low-income persons, but since the Chicago

Board of Elections does not keep a record of registrations by race or income, the only way to gauge the effectiveness of the three groups' combined efforts is by examining recent trends in registration and voter turnout for black and white wards.

Trends in Voter Registration

In 1981, the Chicago City Council redistricted the 50 wards within the city to accommodate the population changes indicated by the 1980 census. The redistricting changed the boundaries of nearly all wards to some degree, to make the population of each approximately 60,000 persons. But in 1982 the U.S. Department of Justice, in conjunction with several minority groups, filed suit in district court charging that the 1981 redistricting plan violated provisions of the Voting Rights Act and the U.S. Constitution. As a result, a new redistricting plan with court-ordered changes went into effect in 1982 after the gubernatorial race.

Under the new plan, blacks became the majority in 2 wards where whites had previously been the majority. That raised the total number of majority-black wards to 19. The Hispanic population also gained majority status in 2 wards, becoming a majority in a total of 4. Figure 2-2, a map of Chicago wards by racial composition, reflects the 1982 redistricting plan.

The following analyses of voter registration and turnout are confined to the aggregate characteristics of wards where either blacks or whites have a population majority of at least 90 percent. The number of wards with a population 90 percent or more white declined after the 1981 redistricting from 7 to 6. After the 1982 court changes, that number remained at 6 (the 13th, 23rd, 36th, 38th, 41st, and 45th wards). The number of wards with a population 90 percent or more black declined after the 1981 redistricting from 14 to 13. After the 1981 court changes, that number declined to 11 (the 2nd, 3rd, 6th, 8th, 16th, 17th, 20th, 21st, 24th, 28th, and 34th wards). No ward (under the 1982 court-ordered changes) had a Hispanic population of more than 75 percent, so a reliable reading on the electoral prefer-

The 12 months preceding the 1983 mayoral election represented a landmark in the 10-year history of Chicago's Special Voter Registration Programs.

ences of those voters would be hard to get. (Registration and turnout in Hispanic wards have been consistently lower than in white and black wards.)

Table 2-2 contains registration rates for black and white wards for the gubernatorial and mayoral elections in 1982 and 1983, respectively. Although the registration rates for both blacks and whites increased progressively during the period of the three elections, the level in black wards remained 5 to 6 percentage points higher than the level in white wards.

Table 2-2
Registration as a Percentage of Voting-Age Population, 1982–1983 (City of Chicago)

	General Election, Governor (1982)	Democratic Primary, Mayor (1983)	General Election, Mayor (1983)
Black wards*	85.0%	87.0%	89.4%
White wards†	79.6	82.1	83.5

*Voting-age population is 90 percent or more black.
†Voting-age population is 90 percent or more white.

For the ... elections in 1982 and 1983, ... the registration rates ... in black wards remained 5 to 6 percentage points higher than the [rates] in white wards.

Comparable rates for elections in 1978 and 1979 are not presented, because reliable data on voting-age population by ward are not available for that period.[11] Newspaper reports from the 1970s, however, indicate that registration levels were generally higher in white wards than in black wards, and the Research and Planning Department of the Chicago Urban League estimates that for the 1980 presidential election, 63.9 percent of the black voting-age population and 73.1 percent of the white voting-age population were registered to vote.

Trends in Voter Turnout

For all three of the major elections in 1982 and 1983, the discrepancy in participation between black and white voters was considerably narrower than it had been in the corresponding elections of 1978 and 1979. The turnout of registered voters in black wards increased by 20 percentage points or more between the elections of 1978 and 1979, on the one hand, and the elections of 1982 and 1983, on the other hand (Table 2-3). Expressed as a percentage of the voting-age population, in the 1982 and 1983 elections black turnout lagged behind white turnout by only a few percentage points (Table 2-4).

In the 1982 gubernatorial election, one of the most striking characteristics of the turnout was the cohesiveness of the vote in black wards. Although turnout per se was higher in white wards, voters in those wards tended to split their support fairly evenly (giving Democratic candidate Adlai Stevenson III the edge). In black wards, however, 89 to 95 percent of the vote went to Stevenson. He received 73 percent of the total vote within Chicago and lost to incumbent Republican James Thompson by less than 1 percentage point statewide.

The pattern of the 1978 gubernatorial vote had been similar, but less pronounced. White wards had generally split their support between the two candidates (incumbent Thompson and Democratic chal-

For all three of the major elections in 1982 and 1983, the discrepancy in participation between black and white voters was considerably narrower than it had been in the corresponding elections of 1978 and 1979.

Table 2-3

Voter Turnout as a Percentage of Registration, 1978–1983 (City of Chicago)

	General Election, Governor (1978)	Democratic Primary, Mayor (1979)	General Election, Mayor (1979)	General Election, Governor (1982)	Democratic Primary, Mayor (1983)	General Election, Mayor (1983)
Black wards*	45.4%	49.0%	51.9%	65.2%	69.4%	78.8%
White wards†	69.2	62.2	68.7	73.0	78.4	85.7

Note: Data are limited to wards with a black or white population of 90% or greater. Because of redistricting and a legal challenge to the Chicago ward map, the number of wards 90% or more black changed in 1981 and again in 1982 after the gubernatorial election.

*Black wards (1978–1979): 2nd, 3rd, 6th, 8th, 9th, 16th, 17th, 20th, 21st, 24th, 27th, 28th, 29th, and 34th.
Black wards (1982): 2nd, 3rd, 6th, 8th, 16th, 17th, 20th, 21st, 24th, 27th, 28th, 29th, and 34th.
Black wards (1983): 2nd, 3rd, 6th, 8th, 16th, 17th, 20th, 21st, 24th, 28th, and 34th.
†White wards (1978–1979): 13th, 23rd, 35th, 36th, 38th, 41st, and 45th.
White wards (1982–1983): 13th, 23rd, 36th, 38th, 41st, and 45th.

Table 2-4
Voter Turnout as a Percentage of Voting-Age Population, 1982–1983 (City of Chicago)

	General Election, Governor (1982)	Democratic Primary, Mayor (1983)	General Election, Mayor (1983)
Black wards*	55.4%	60.4%	70.4%
White wards†	58.1	64.4	71.6

*Voting-age population is 90 percent or more black.
†Voting-age population is 90 percent or more white.

In the 1982 gubernatorial election, . . . black turnout for Stevenson was remarkable: . . .

lenger Michael Bakalis); support for Bakalis in black wards had ranged from 64 percent to 89 percent, and he received 59 percent of the total vote within the city.

In commenting on the November 1982 gubernatorial election, many members of the media failed to see what the cohesiveness of the black vote implied for Democratic mayoral politics in the coming year. In interpreting the overwhelming support blacks gave to Democratic candidate Stevenson, they emphasized traditional divisions between urban blacks and the Republican party. From that perspective, President Reagan's policies (at the federal level, and as filtered through the state administration of Governor Thompson) were seen as the primary impetus to black electoral participation.

This focus on the repercussions of national political programs, however, deflected attention from an important characteristic of local voting behavior: blacks tend to vote as a bloc for the candidate most closely identified or associated with their interests. Black turnout for Stevenson was remarkable—yet, it was hard to see in what way he was identified or associated with black interests. He had not taken any strong public stands on minority issues; like his opponent, he was criticized for conducting a lackluster campaign; and his strongest selling points were his liberal reputation and his criticism of Reagan, neither of which, alone or in combination, appeared sufficient to motivate the degree of electoral mobilization that in fact occurred. How, then, did blacks see him as representing their interests? Lu Palmer asserted that "black people were practicing up for February 22nd," the date of the mayoral primary.

In the previous Democratic mayoral primary, in 1979, Jane Byrne had won with 51 percent of the total vote and had carried almost all the wards that were 90 percent or more black (with a level of support ranging from 33 percent to 79 percent). In the 1983 primary, however, she received only 33 percent of the total vote. Richard M. Daley received 30 percent, and Harold Washington received 37 percent. Eighty percent of the ballots for Washington were cast by voters in wards that were 50 percent or more black.

Voting in the three-way primary followed racial and ethnic lines (Figure 2-3). Washington carried all the wards that were at least 50 percent black plus the multi-racial 1st ward, where blacks composed 45 percent of the population, Hispanics 21 percent, whites 23 percent, and other racial groups 11 percent. In wards that were 90 percent or more black, he received 77 to 87 percent of the vote. Balloting in white-majority wards split between Daley, who carried the predominantly Irish Southwest Side, and Byrne, who carried the predominantly Polish Northwest Side and the North Side and Lakefront areas.

The black vote in the mayoral general election two months later was monolithic, and the racial pattern of voter support resembled that in the mayoral primary (Figure 2-4). Washington again carried the multiracial 1st ward and all the black wards; in the heavily black wards he received 99 percent of the vote, with the exception of the 2nd ward, where his support was 97 percent. In addition, he gained the 22nd and 31st wards, both Hispanic and both adjacent to predominantly black communities. The vote in another Hispanic ward, the 25th, split 49 to 51 percent between Washington and his Republican opponent, Bernard Epton.

Of the political contests discussed in this analysis, the only ones in which bloc voting was evident in

"Black people were practicing up for" . . . *the mayoral primary.*

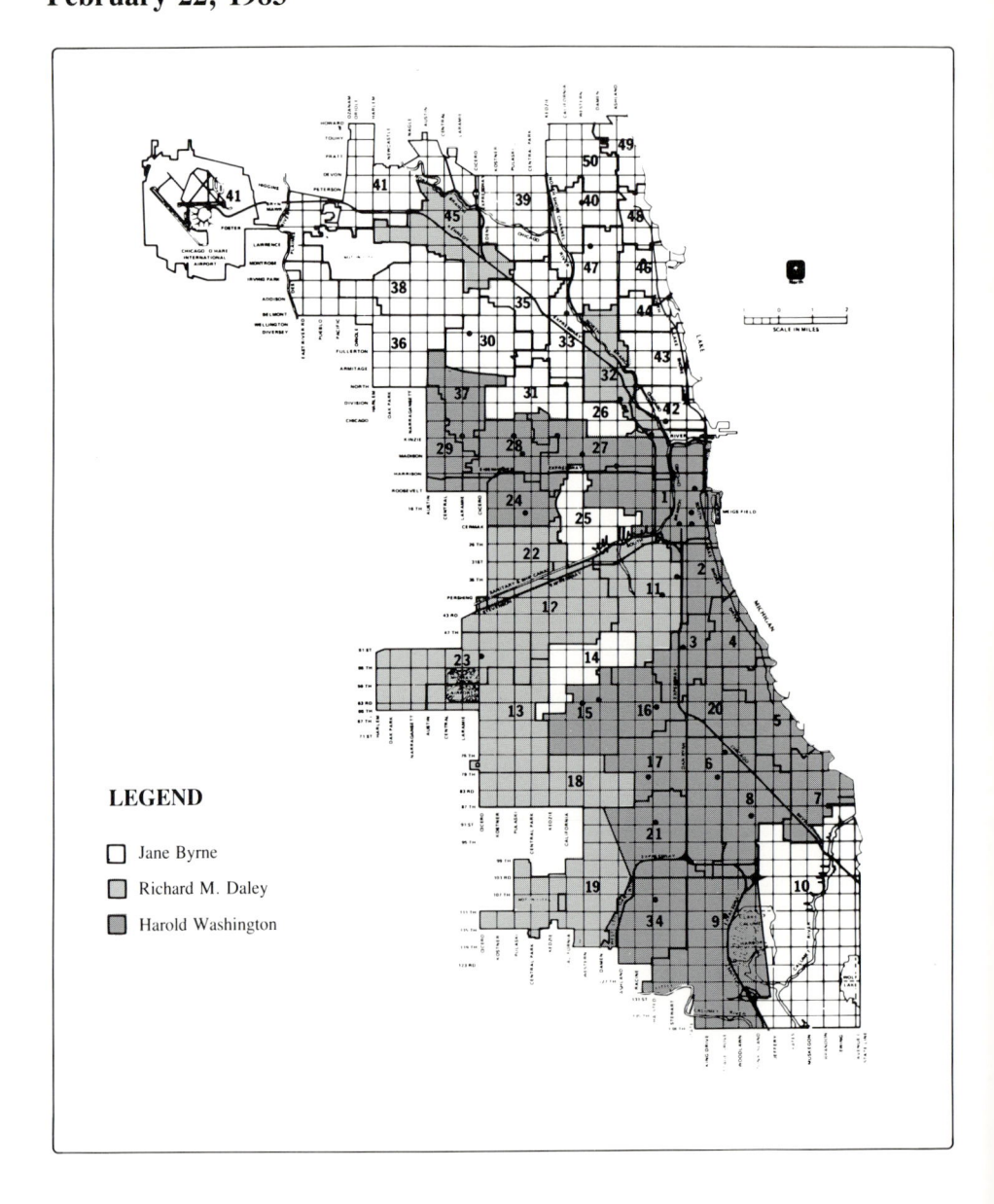

Figure 2-3
Wards Won by Candidates in Chicago Mayoral Primary Election, February 22, 1983

LEGEND

☐ Jane Byrne
▨ Richard M. Daley
▨ Harold Washington

Figure 2-4
Wards Won by Candidates in Chicago Mayoral General Election, April 12, 1983

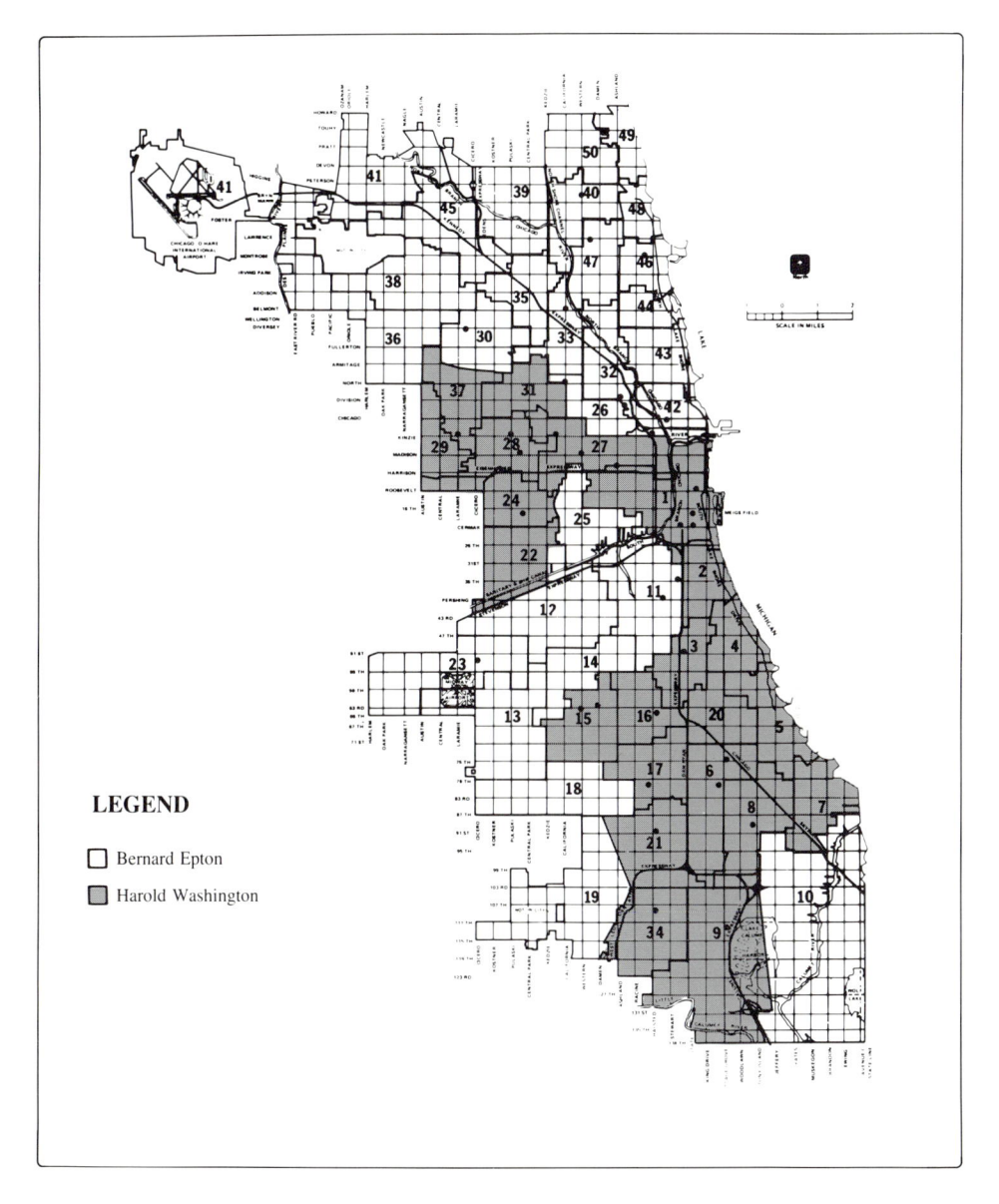

LEGEND

☐ Bernard Epton
▓ Harold Washington

heavily white wards were the 1979 and 1983 mayoral general elections. In 1983, Epton received 93 to 96 percent of the vote in the heavily white wards, despite the Democratic party's long-standing preeminence in local politics in Chicago. The presence of a black candidate in a major election obviously generated an extremely high degree of polarization among both the black and the white electorates.

Conclusion

Professor Charles V. Hamilton, in an article published in 1977, suggested that the attempts to increase voter registration and election day turnout in many black communities have traditionally been two distinct operations, conducted by separate types of organizations.[12] Nonpartisan groups have taken responsibility for voter registration activities, commonly defined as voter education programs, whereas get-out-the-vote drives have been principally the province of labor unions and party organizations. Because of this division of labor, the relationship between voter registration and election day turnout activity has been minimal.

In contrast, the voter outreach project in Chicago in 1982-1983 was comprehensive and broad-based. Voter registration, voter education, and get-out-the-vote activities were successfully combined into a single movement with four distinct elements:

The voter outreach project in Chicago in 1982–1983 was comprehensive and broad-based.

- existing community organizations developed an effective grassroots operation;
- legal action was taken to increase the number of registration opportunities available to minorities and the poor;
- a sophisticated media campaign was designed to reach the greatest number of potential voters; and
- the local political climate stimulated black interest in politics.

In combination, these four elements made a black mayoral candidacy viable and ultimately successful.

List of Persons Interviewed

Frances Bullock, Soft Sheen Products

Walter "Slim" Coleman, president, Heart of Uptown Coalition

Danny Davis, alderman, Chicago City Council

Thomas Johnson, attorney, Legal Assistance Foundation, Chicago

Lu Palmer, Chicago Black United Communities (CBUC)

Lawrence Saunders, director, Social Services Department, Chicago Urban League

James A. Thomas, attorney, Cornfield and Feldman, Chicago

Emma Young, Soft Sheen Products

Endnotes

1. Eric Hyde and Roger Fox, *Why Chicago Blacks Do Not Register and Vote* (Chicago: Chicago Urban League, 1981), p. 21.

2. Robert Davis, "Poor Gate Laid to Rain and Boycott," *Chicago Tribune* (December 14, 1982).

3. Under Illinois law, voter registration programs had to be nonpartisan or not affiliated with any political party or candidate.

4. On November 10, 1982, the day Washington announced his candidacy, Illinois Bell Telephone Company withdrew its sponsorship of "Lu's Notebook" because of Palmer's alleged partisan politics. "Lu's Notebook" had been broadcast daily on four radio stations: WVON (AM), WJPC (AM), WBEE

(AM), and WGCI (FM). As of 1983, Palmer had only one outlet, WXOL (AM), where he hosted "On Target" from 10 p.m. to midnight, Monday and Thursday.

5. The source for this narrative of POWER's legal actions is the *Corrected Brief of Plaintiffs—Appellees*, prepared by the Legal Assistance Foundation of Chicago (Trial Court No. 82-C-7144; United States District Court of the Northern District of Illinois, Eastern Division).

6. Ibid., p. 10.

7. Ibid., p. 12.

8. This information on the history of VOTE Community was obtained from the *Voter Registration Manual* prepared by Soft Sheen Products, Inc. (1983).

9. Robinson served as Washington's first campaign manager during the 1983 primary election campaign.

10. *Special Voter Registration Programs: Yearly Progress Report* (Chicago Board of Elections Commissioners, 1983). As the figures indicate, library programs remain one of the most effective forms of voter outreach within the city of Chicago. The Board of Elections implemented a special outreach registration program at public libraries throughout the city in 1979, and between then and March 1983 that program accounted for more than 143,000 registrations.

11. The city of Chicago has not published data on voting-age population for city wards as they existed in 1980, before the 1981 redistricting.

12. Charles V. Hamilton, "Voter Registration Drives and Turnout: A Report on the Harlem Electorate," *Political Science Quarterly*, 92 (Spring 1977), 43-46.

3. BUILDING A BASE OF VOLUNTEERS IN PHILADELPHIA

Sandra Featherman

In 1983, W. Wilson Goode became the first black mayor in Philadelphia's history. During the campaign, his biggest obstacle was the May 17 Democratic primary against former Mayor Frank L. Rizzo. However, by using the infrastructure created during several years of massive black registration efforts and combining it with the services of a large number of volunteers, Goode's staff conducted a registration drive that succeeded in adding nearly 90,000 newly registered black citizens to the voting rolls before the primary election. Since Goode won that election by 59,417 votes, the large number of newly registered voters may well have provided his margin of victory.

Goode's opponent in the primary also made a substantial registration effort: some 83,000 additional whites were added to the Democratic rolls before the primary, and most were expected to support Rizzo. Nearly half of the new white Democratic registrants had previously been registered as Republicans and had been actively recruited to switch parties in order to swell the ranks of Rizzo supporters in the Democratic primary election. (Some of the new white voters probably voted for Goode, whereas almost none of the new black registrants voted for Rizzo. Thus, the nearly equal numbers of new black and new white Democratic registrants did not cancel each other out.)

In the primary, Rizzo claimed to have been supportive of the black community in his earlier terms as mayor, appointing many blacks to government jobs. However, his campaign was clearly aimed at white voters, and in black areas he received only about 5 percent of the vote. After the primary, Rizzo endorsed Goode for the general election.

Goode's staff conducted a registration drive that succeeded in adding nearly 90,000 newly registered black citizens to the voting rolls before the primary election.

Goode won the general election handily, securing 55 percent of the vote in a three-person race. He garnered 97 percent of the black vote and 22.5 percent of the white vote, more than enough to glide to an easy victory, although Goode forces worried to the end that they might not draw a large black turnout once Rizzo was no longer on the ballot as a catalyst for that turnout. As it turned out, proportionally more blacks than whites voted in the general election (in relation to each race's voting-age population).

Background

The dramatic increase in black registration in Philadelphia in 1983 was the result of several factors all coming together:

- the legal requirements for registration had changed in 1976;
- elections in 1976 and 1978 had already stimulated blacks' interest in politics and led to the creation of an infrastructure for organizing registration drives;
- opportunity seemed to be knocking; and
- a desirable candidate was available.

The Legal Requirements for Registration

Most important was the change in the registration laws of Pennsylvania that took effect in August 1976. Fred Voigt, director of the Committee of Seventy (a civic watchdog agency particularly concerned with the integrity of the electoral system), attributes the wave of increases in black registration that took place between 1976 and 1983 chiefly to the new laws, which made it no longer mandatory to register in person. Nonpersonal, or mail-in, registration was permissible from 1976 on.

Before August 1976, a citizen who wished to register to vote generally had to go downtown to the Registration Commission in City Hall, bringing suitable identification (such as a birth certificate or a driver's license). The alternative of traveling regis-

Before August 1976, a citizen who wished to register to vote generally had to go downtown to the Registration Commission in City Hall.

trars was available, particularly before elections, but the traveling registrars' schedules were erratic and their assignments were alleged to be politically motivated. (Assignments were made by the Registration Commission, generally at the direction of the Democratic party leadership.) In any case, few persons knew when or where to find the traveling registrars. The difficulty was particularly severe in low-income neighborhoods.

But after August 1976 a citizen could register by mail, using "official nonpersonal voter registration application cards." Those registration application cards, which can be filled out in minutes at a person's home or anywhere else, must be supplied by the secretary of the commonwealth to any person or organized group upon request. The cards are self-mailers for which no stamps are necessary, since the state pays postage.[1] (Persons wishing to register in person may still do so.)

After August 1976 a citizen could register by mail.

The card is relatively straightforward. The only things a person needs to list are name, party, address, sex, height, hair color, eye color, skin color, need for voting assistance (if any), whether this is a new registration, a change of party, or a change of address, and whether the person has ever before registered to vote.

The card warns that false information is punishable by a fine and/or imprisonment. Although a few local politicians have gone to jail for filling out forms for nonexistent persons, fraud of this type does not appear to be a major problem.

Duplicate Registration. Unintentional duplicate registration, however, is another story. There the intent is not to defraud, but apparently to ensure that one is really registered in time to vote. In Philadelphia, if someone is uncertain that previously completed forms have been validated, that person may legally register more than once. When someone registers by mail, the registration application states that the local county board of elections will return to that person, by nonforwardable mail and within 10 days, a voter notification stub indicating that the person is officially registered. Persons not receiving a notifi-

In Philadelphia, if someone is uncertain that previously completed forms have been validated, that person may legally register more than once.

cation stub within 10 days may re-register to be sure of having the right to vote in the forthcoming election. (Duplicate registration may also occur when someone who has moved within the city registers at the new location without his or her name's being removed from voter records at the old location.) Duplicate registration entails no penalty as long as a registrant does not attempt to vote more than once—and duplicate voting is something few observers in Philadelphia believe to be common.

City election officials purge the lists of duplications in several ways: by using nonforwardable postcards that must be returned by the U.S. Postal Service if delivery is unsuccessful; by comparing new names and addresses with those already on file; and by asking political workers or citizens to report changes in a voter's place of residence. Before the 1983 primary election, however, duplicates plagued the registration lists more than usual. Officials had fallen behind in their data processing at the same time that massive numbers of people were registering for the first time.

An indication of the scope of the problem is that if both the registration figures for May 1983 and the 1980 census data were accurate, then almost every black person of voting age in Philadelphia who could hold a pen must have been registered. The final count in May 1983 indicated a total of 436,298 blacks registered to vote—and the total black adult population of the city in 1980 was listed as 433,964.[2]

The figures indicate that duplicate registration may have been most prevalent among black males, 104 percent of whom apparently registered to vote. The figure for black females was 99 percent; for all whites, 83 percent; and for all "others" (a self-defined category that includes Asians, some Hispanics, and persons who do not identify themselves by color on the registration form), 73 percent.

Deputy Commissioner of Registration John Furey has indicated that in the future he hopes to have registrants use their social security numbers for registration numbers and that he also hopes to use computer programs, which will enable his staff to scan quickly for duplications. As of mid-1983, however, such computer programs were not operational.

Previous Elections of Interest to Blacks

Also contributing to the dramatic rise in the proportion of blacks registered to vote were two earlier political contests (in 1976 and 1978) that had stimulated the interest of blacks and led to the creation of an infrastructure for organizing and conducting registration drives. In those two earlier election years, the number of black registrants in Philadelphia—and the black share of total registration—increased substantially (see Table 3-1).

Table 3-1
Growth of Black Voter Registration in Philadelphia, 1975–1983

Year	Black Registration*	Total Registration	Black Proportion of Total
1975	252,129	865,007	29.1%
1976	313,816	972,855	32.3
1977	301,467	934,213	32.3
1978	391,461	1,041,799	37.6
1979	369,257	986,930	37.4
1980	371,295	996,587	37.2
1981	362,455	972,992	37.2
1982	347,303	941,010	36.9
1983	436,423	1,114,032	39.2

*Before 1982, registrants were coded as colored, white, or foreign-born (a category that was basically white). In 1982, the coding was changed to black, white, and other.

Data compiled from Philadelphia Registration Commission reports and print-outs, 1975 through August 1983.

If both the registration figures for May 1983 and the 1980 census data were accurate, then almost every black person of voting age in Philadelphia who could hold a pen must have been registered.

One of the two contests was the 1976 presidential election. Jimmy Carter, running against President Gerald Ford, received a great deal of support from the black community in Philadelphia. The coupling of a presidential election of interest to blacks with the relaxation of registration requirements led an additional 62,000 black voters to register, for an increase of nearly 25 percent in black registration.

Since the total gain in registration that year was 108,000, blacks constituted 57 percent of the aggregate registration increase.

Clearly, both the presidential election and the legal changes had greater impact on the black community than on the white. Nevertheless, in 1976 blacks were still underregistered relative to their share of the population, constituting approximately 36 to 37 percent of the city's population but only 32 percent of those registered to vote.

For the other election of importance to blacks, in 1978, black registration increased by just under 90,000—an astonishing 84 percent of the total gain of 107,586 in that year. This made blacks 37.6 percent of the registered voters, about equal to the black share of the population of the city. The issue that spurred this increase in registration was a referendum item, a question on the ballot asking voters to approve a change in the city charter to allow a mayor to serve more than two terms.

For all practical purposes, this was a referendum on Frank Rizzo, the incumbent mayor. His second term would end the following year, and he sought to change the charter so he could run for a third term. Rizzo had never been popular in the black community (in the 1975 general election he had won only 34 percent of the black vote) and blacks were not expected to support his effort to change the charter, but the depth of their opposition was unexpected by many. Blacks joined forces with liberal whites and even many moderate whites to defeat the referendum overwhelmingly. Only 3 percent of the black voters supported the charter change; 97 percent voted "No."

The catalyst in that election may well have been Rizzo's famous "vote white" statement, in which he reportedly said that "whites would vote white" and added, "and right-thinking blacks." Blacks throughout the city were enraged. Ministers took to their pulpits to urge parishioners to register and vote on the referendum, and those efforts apparently had a major impact on both registration and turnout. Before the election, a white former registration official predicted that the new black registrants would never

Two earlier political contests . . . had stimulated the interest of blacks and led to the creation of an infrastructure for organizing and conducting registration drives.

bother to vote. He said that registration—much of which took place outside churches and in highly trafficked areas—had been made as easy as signing petitions, but that voting required one to find out the polling place, get there, and wait in line to cast a ballot. In fact, black turnout in that election was quite high for an off-year election—about 63 percent of the number registered. Turnout as a proportion of all registered voters, black and white, was only slightly higher—68 percent.[3]

The charter referendum did more than increase the number of registered blacks. It also gave rise to a sense of electoral strength within the black community. With the charter referendum, politics in Philadelphia decisively changed.

The charter referendum . . . gave rise to a sense of electoral strength within the black community.

Opportunity and a Desirable Candidate

The following year a black attorney, Charles Bowser, came within 44,000 votes of winning the Democratic mayoral primary election against William Green, who went on to win the general election in a three-way race against a white Republican (former U.S. Attorney David Marstan) and a black third-party candidate (City Councilman Lucien Blackwell). During the general election campaign Green promised that, if elected, he would appoint a black to the position of managing director, the top administrative post under the mayor. Green honored his promise with the appointment of W. Wilson Goode as the city's managing director.

By mid-1982, Green had not yet initiated any re-election efforts and his intentions were still unknown. Efforts were begun to draft Goode as the Democratic nominee, but not until Green declared he would not run again for mayor did Goode participate in these efforts. After resigning his position of managing director as the city charter required him to do,[4] he entered the race.

The 1983 primary campaign pitted Goode against Frank Rizzo, who was trying for a comeback, and blacks once more responded in large numbers to efforts to register them: another 90,000 potential black voters registered. In May when the primary was held, blacks represented 39.2 percent of all regis-

> "*You would have had to put up barricades to keep people in the black community from voting.*"

tered voters—greater than their 37.8 percent share of the city's population—and, most importantly, they now constituted 44 percent of the registered Democrats in the city.

The numbers helped generate a perception that a black could be elected at the top of the ticket. The black community had come close with Charles Bowser, but this time people sensed that a black could go all the way, particularly since the black in question—Wilson Goode—had many admirers and potential supporters in the white community. Such a perception undoubtedly led many previously alienated or uninterested blacks first to register and then to vote. As Lenore Berson, former chairperson of the Philadelphia chapter of Americans for Democratic Action and a member of the Goode campaign staff, declared, "You would have had to put up barricades to keep people in the black community from voting."

Gregg Naylor, the Goode registration coordinator, said that the strongest force motivating black registration was the desire to vote for Goode on election day. "You can't vote for Wilson Goode unless you are registered to vote" was the message sent out from headquarters.

Organizational Dynamics

Many of the persons and groups involved in Goode's voter education and registration effort were also involved in his get-out-the-vote campaign. Unlike numerous other political campaigns, this one used a core of grassroots volunteers, building on an infrastructure of community organization workers, who not only did nonpartisan registration but also later worked at the polls as partisans to bring out the vote. The nonpartisan registration efforts were particularly important to the Goode campaign because they could be targeted at black neighborhoods wherever registration was too low, using tax-exempt foundation or corporate grants or public dollars otherwise unavailable to the Goode campaign.

Although the Goode staff could not officially coordinate many of the outside efforts, since the Goode campaign was partisan and many of the registration efforts were nonpartisan, unofficially much coordination did take place. And because an overwhelming majority of blacks were expected to register Democratic and vote for Goode, nonpartisan registration efforts directed at the black community were as useful to the Goode campaign as were partisan efforts, even in the absence of coordination.

Nonpartisan groups that made substantial contributions to the registration effort included the Urban Coalition, which was noted as playing a particularly valuable role; the Urban League; and community-based civic and neighborhood groups. Many college campuses (Philadelphia contains more than 50 colleges and other institutions of higher education) also ran registration drives, which were seen as marginal but helpful.

Registration Efforts

Naylor set up 10 area field offices throughout the city to serve 38 of Philadelphia's 66 wards. Areas were selected for field offices on the basis of several factors: where the black population was, where supporting ward leaders who requested field office support were, and where several wards' efforts could be coordinated. Of the 38 wards served, many were overwhelmingly black; some had substantial pockets of blacks; and several were white wards expected to support Goode. By the May primary, 30 wards showed an absolute majority of black registrants and, in another 7, between 25 and 50 percent of the registrants were black.

Targeting the Unregistered. Registration was the field offices' main responsibility, and each office was assigned a registration quota. Each field staff director had to turn in registration applications to Naylor, who coordinated the effort and monitored each field office's performance.

In organizing their registration effort, the members of Goode's campaign staff started with the 1980 census data. They compared total black regis-

Many of the persons and groups involved in Goode's voter education and registration effort were also involved in his get-out-the-vote campaign.

tration with the official census count of the black population to come up with the number of unregistered blacks, and added to that figure the number of blacks who had turned 18 since 1980. This yielded an estimate of 80,000-112,000 unregistered blacks in the 38 wards targeted for registration efforts. The campaign's goal was to register 85,000 persons. (The goal was exceeded, since the campaign brought in 115,000 new black registrants altogether, with a net gain in registered black voters—after allowing for those who had moved away, died, or let their status lapse—of approximately 90,000.)

It is easier to identify areas of potential black registration in Pennsylvania than in some other states, since Pennsylvania includes race as an identifying characteristic on registration applications. And the city of Philadelphia compiles registration statistics for each ward and electoral division by race. Campaign workers can compare census tract numbers for black adults with the numbers registered to vote in electoral divisions within the tracts. Block statistics are even more useful, since some electoral divisions cross census tracts.

After the election, Naylor indicated that more information had been needed on voter registration as it relates to low-income and minority populations, with particular emphasis on what motivates those groups. He would have welcomed such material, which could have sensitized his registrars to the reasons for traditional underregistration and low turnout in low-income, minority areas.

Registration was the field offices' main responsibility, and each office was assigned a registration quota.

Using Volunteers. Each of the 10 field offices was served by one paid staff person and substantial numbers of volunteers. Among the volunteers, many were black mid-level professionals: school personnel (both administrators and teachers), social workers, lawyers, employees of nonprofit organizations, and people associated with school parent groups and with church groups. They not only carried out the volunteer effort, but they also helped to manage it.

The reason volunteers were used heavily to augment political leaders is that the latter did not have the kinds of strong ward organizations they could fall back on. The political strength of blacks in the city had developed so recently and was so fluid that the political loyalties on which machines are usually built were less potent in the black sections of Philadelphia than in areas where long-standing political relationships had developed. Black registration as a whole might have increased 42 percent from 1975 through 1983, but the turnover of individuals who were registered from year to year was high. Most of the gain was due to the new registration of old residents and of newly eligible young voters, and some of the gain simply reflected change caused by residential relocation. Thus, even if the total number of registrants had remained fixed, probably over half of all blacks registered for the primary election would either not have been registered at all eight years earlier or would not have been registered in the same voting divisions (the local equivalent of precincts).

In addition to lacking strong local organizations, black ward leaders also lacked a tradition of directing registration efforts. Registration efforts in the black community in Philadelphia historically had been led by black ministers speaking from the pulpit, sometimes supported by white liberal groups. Moreover, the two major parties, although supporting black registration efforts with rhetoric, had rarely given much practical support. Many white political leaders considered the local black vote to be predictable in terms of delivery (to the Democrats) but unreliable in terms of turnout.

Finally, many black ward leaders had been picked by the white leadership rather than by the black voters in their respective wards. One knowledgeable person claimed that the old black leaders were not interested in registering new voters who might challenge their leadership, but that the new black leaders—people like Congressman William Gray, City Councilman John White, state legislator Chaka Fattah, and others—increased their support by means of strong registration drives.

Relationships to Outside Groups

Goode's campaign staff (like Rizzo's) claimed that it had no relationship at all to national registration efforts. Except in fund-raising campaigns, the

Except in fund-raising campaigns, the Goode staff assiduously avoided ties to anything outside the Philadelphia area.

> *Since the party was ineffective, each side worked with its own ward leaders.*

Goode staff assiduously avoided ties to anything outside the Philadelphia area. For example, after the Reverend Jesse Jackson made a widely publicized appearance in the city (and Rizzo, apparently to stimulate a backlash, then referred to Jackson's remarks about registering blacks and accused Jackson of supporting the Palestine Liberation Organization and Muammar Qadhafi of Libya), Goode's staff stated that they had not invited Jackson to come and that extraneous issues should not be injected into the local campaign.

Officials of the local government were helpful to the Goode registration efforts, according to several sources in the Goode campaign. The mayor supported Goode, as did the chief registration commissioner. And since Goode had been managing director of the city, he had extensive contacts in city government. Government data and registration forms were regularly made available to his people.

The local Democratic party organization stayed neutral. In effect, there was no party, just a fragmented set of ward leaders, some lining up with Rizzo and some with Goode. In a bitterly contested fight for chairperson of the Democratic City Committee, Edgar Campbell, an elderly, long-time black politician supported by Goode, was named acting chairperson, and a Rizzo supporter, Joseph Smith, became permanent chairperson. Because his victory was narrow and the coalition was fragile, Smith, as new chairperson, stated that the City Committee would be neutral. The decline of its influence over nominations had been in the making for over a decade—a decade of Rizzo vs. anti-Rizzo splits in the ranks.

The Battle of Endorsements

Since the party was ineffective, each side worked with its own ward leaders. In wards where leaders did not support Goode, the Goode campaign worked with friendly party workers.

Official party endorsements had been the norm in Philadelphia. Without them, candidates below the top of the ticket floundered and became highly dependent on endorsements from either Goode or

Rizzo. These endorsements meant that the endorsed candidates' names were printed on the Goode or Rizzo "ballot" distributed to voters. In fact, every candidate who went on to win election to local office was included on one of those two ballots. Goode's coattails were particularly long, carrying to victory most of the local candidates who had appeared on his sample ballot.

Goode won the endorsement war for two reasons. First, he made his selections early, whereas Rizzo held back on some races until the last week. Second, Goode mailed his "official" ballot to households with registered voters in the areas deemed supportive of his candidacy (black and liberal white wards) and urged that voters take the sample ballot with them to the polls and use only that ballot, called the Official Goode Ballot, as a guide in voting. Goode's mailer cautioned voters to accept no other sample ballots at the polls—a precaution made necessary by the near-anarchy among some ward leaders. With the Democratic City Committee not pushing them to endorse an official slate, many ward leaders were fashioning their own slates and cutting deals with individual candidates, often in return for "street money" for election day costs.

Goode's ploy worked. Particularly in many black areas, voters came to the polls with the Goode ballot, voted for its slate, and helped to nominate quite a few new faces—who owed their political success to endorsement by Wilson Goode.

A number of candidates supported by Goode worked actively to help the registration effort. Sources among Rizzo's staff stated that Goode's candidates did a much better registration job than Rizzo's candidates did. One Rizzo aide acknowledged that Goode's candidates were "more committed, more dedicated, and worked harder" on voter registration.

[Goode's registration coordinator] went after every possible unregistered black.

Outreach Activities

The Goode Campaign

Naylor went after every possible unregistered black, targeting potential new registrants in areas where polls, demographics, or friendly ward leaders had indicated that new registrants would be Goode supporters. Naylor's people made little effort to urge new registrants to register as Democrats, assuming that most blacks who selected a party *would* register as Democrats. An effort was made, however, to remind persons not to register as nonpartisan. Because many city residents who work for branches of the government mistakenly believe they must register as nonpartisan, the voter education effort stressed that government workers could register by party and that *only* persons registered by party could vote in the party's primary election.

According to Naylor, the most successful strategy was to set up high-visibility registration tables not only at supermarkets and shopping malls in black neighborhoods, but also outside public assistance offices and check-cashing establishments. Also important were rallies held at schools, churches, and malls, and the person-to-person efforts of an army of volunteers abetted by some supportive political leaders. The least productive and least used activities were door-to-door projects, which Naylor said were "slow, tedious, and took a large number of people." The Goode registration project used no direct mail.

The theme stressed by the Goode campaigners was simply that people had to register in order to vote for Goode on May 17. Goode himself helped immensely by being highly visible and generating much media attention. Indeed, as Lenore Berson indicated, television was a critical factor. On the television news shows, members of the black community continually saw Goode, a well-known black, running for mayor. They realized that many whites supported Goode, and they regularly heard about polls indicating that Goode could or would win.

As Naylor put it, the black registration efforts were intended to proceed quietly so as not to alarm the other side or "get folks stirred up." Naylor did not, for example, purchase space in the black newspaper, *The Tribune*. The Goode campaign purchased spots urging blacks to register and vote on only one black radio station and only during the last several

The most successful strategy was to set up high-visibility registration tables not only at supermarkets and shopping malls in black neighborhoods, but also outside public assistance offices and check-cashing establishments.

days of the registration period. The phone number of Goode headquarters was given for those who wanted additional information. Regardless, the black media pushed voter registration strongly.

The one disquieting note was a rumor—which the staff tried to dispel—that the Goode campaign was registering only blacks. The campaign was concerned that it not alienate potential white support by appearing to be concerned simply with black voters. An incident occurred during registration that also brought some negative publicity to the Goode effort. Goode was accused of organizing a drive to register persons at the Philadelphia prisons. While Pennsylvania law no longer prohibits prisoners from voting, the general public expressed some outrage that the votes of lawbreakers would be reached for by any candidate. The fact that the prisons in question were largely populated by blacks added a racial aspect to the issue. The supposed effort to register prisoners got a lot of coverage in the media, but Goode denied that he was sponsoring such an effort. In fact, although his campaign staff may not have conducted prison registration officially, a volunteer group, Educators for Goode, held a meeting at Goode headquarters during which the group's plans to conduct such registration were mentioned.

The Goode primary campaign raised about $2 million, but much of it came in during the last few weeks, after voter registration was closed. (Registration in Pennsylvania closes 30 days before an election.) Naylor was not given a formal budget for his registration program. Instead, costs were supported as necessary. Each field office had at most one paid staff person; several of the offices used donated space; and each office had just one phone. Naylor estimates that from late January through April 18, when registration closed, he spent a maximum of $50,000 on personnel, literature, distribution of material, and phones.

Goode himself helped immensely by being highly visible and generating much media attention.

The Rizzo Campaign

The Rizzo people, unlike the Goode people, could not afford the luxury of much nonpartisan registration. A lot of their effort, according to Buddy

Each field office had at most one paid staff person; several of the offices used donated space; and each office had just one phone.

Pitts, who coordinated Rizzo's registration efforts, was spent trying to get Republican registrants in white areas who were perceived as friendly to Rizzo to re-register as Democrats. Pitts sought 20,000 changeovers. In fact, the Rizzo campaign signed up almost 40,000 changeovers plus nearly 45,000 new Democrats, for a net gain of roughly 83,000. But Pitts had to monitor and control new registrations brought in by his contacts to be sure they were likely to be Rizzo supporters. Pitts said that he questioned sources extensively when receiving new registrants from areas deemed liberal, but that even possibly unfriendly names were processed.

Like the Goode people, the Rizzo people used shopping centers. At one mall in the northeastern part of the city they registered 1,000 persons a week. The most successful project used by Pitts, however, was the mailer. Thousands of recipients of the mailer called Pitts's office; volunteers then visited the callers and either registered them or changed their registration to Democrat.

Some Rizzo staffers say the Rizzo volunteer effort never reached its full potential. Less than 1,000 volunteers materialized; several thousand would have been normal in a city the size of Philadelphia.

The underlying message on the Rizzo side—never explicit but always implicit—was that this was a black-white contest. There was no need to emphasize the point, and neither race nor Goode was ever mentioned in any of the Rizzo registration materials. Pitts acknowledged that some of the Rizzo volunteers on the street might have used race as an issue, but in all official printed and broadcast material, the Rizzo side, like the Goode side, sought carefully to avoid putting out racially selective or loaded messages that would steer supporters to the opposition (although each side counted on bringing out what it saw as its own natural constituency).

The Rizzo people estimated that they spent between $100,000 and $150,000 on registration. Pitts claimed that $50,000 to $60,000 alone was spent on direct mail urging Republicans to change their registration. Much of the rest went for advertising, phones, and out-of-pocket expenses for volunteers.

Effectiveness

Registration

Supporters and opponents generally agree that the Goode registration drive was highly successful. It brought in more than 115,000 new black registrants and, after duplicate registrations and people who had left the rolls were accounted for, it netted around 90,000 additional registered voters. By the May primary, of the 436,423 blacks who were registered, 91 percent (or more than 395,000) were registered as Democrats. Slightly more than 26,700, or 6 percent, were registered as Republicans, and the remaining 3 percent (14,500) were registered as nonpartisan or members of minor parties.

Of the nearly 648,000 registered whites, after shifts to the Democratic party 74 percent were registered as Democrats (about 479,500) and 23 percent (about 147,000) as Republicans.

To evaluate the effectiveness of the voter registration project, Naylor regularly checked field office reports against quotas. No modifications or changes in tactics were developed as a result of such feedback. In general, the effort was so successful that changes seemed unwarranted. The Rizzo effort likewise did not change. "The numbers spoke for themselves," Pitts said. "We were more elated each week."

Duplicate Registrations. If success in the registration drive had been measured simply by the number of registration forms generated, both sides could have prided themselves on even more of an accomplishment. A total of 250,000 forms were turned in to the Registration Commission.[5] Estimates of the number of duplicate registrations in this primary were impressionistic. Normally, running totals are kept, and estimates of strike-offs (applications eliminated because they are found to be duplicative, erroneous, fictitious, etc.) are available. John Furey, the deputy commissioner of registration, had no such figures available at the time this research was conducted, because the city was in the process of changing its data retrieval vendors. Complications

Supporters and opponents generally agree that the Goode registration drive was highly successful.

arose, list purgings fell behind, and totals were not generated. Neither the individual nor any group collecting or turning in the registration forms was penalized for duplication. In fact, new mail-in registration laws shifted the burden for controlling duplication from the individual voter or campaign personnel to the government.

Many persons registered more than once because overzealous volunteers in both camps urged persons who were unsure of their status to fill out a second form to avoid taking a chance on being unable to vote on election day. Most observers thought duplicate registration was much greater among blacks than among whites, although substantial duplication is presumed to have taken place among both groups.

Pitts claimed he tightly checked new registrations turned in to him for duplications until the last two weeks of the registration period, when he urged those people who had not received official confirmation of their registration to fill out the forms again and send them in. Naylor did not review forms for duplication. His efforts were geared to using his resources to get the unregistered on the voting rolls.

Some of the people interviewed thought that the Rizzo staff might have had better control over duplicate registrations than the Goode staff did, not only because the Rizzo staff checked the new registrations that were turned in but also because they worked through seasoned political regulars who knew their neighbors well and checked the precinct street lists (the precinct roll of registered voters, by address) to see who was or was not registered. The staff could then direct their energies more efficiently.

The Goode effort was more scattershot. Street lists were not used, and screening efforts were not made. Had the Goode campaign tried to screen registrants, the effort probably would have been costly and wasteful of the staff's time and resources.

Furthermore, as Fred Voigt of the Committee of Seventy pointed out, registration drives, quotas, and reward systems led Goode volunteers and staff to concentrate on generating more and more filled-out

> *Most observers thought duplicate registration was much greater among blacks than among whites, although substantial duplication is presumed to have taken place among both groups.*

registration forms rather than on ensuring the bottom line—getting the unregistered to register and then getting them to the polls. But according to Voigt, what ultimately matters is votes, not the sheer number of forms turned in.

Voigt told the story of a citywide group that had received a grant several years earlier to conduct a registration drive. As one of many groups conducting such drives, this organization would not have been able to take sole credit for net gains in registration. So instead they counted and reported the number of applications they generated and turned in to City Hall. Voigt feels that such an emphasis gives rise to internal pressure that, in turn, produces overregistration through duplication.

Since the effort by the Goode campaign to register blacks was hugely successful, Goode originally intended to continue his registration efforts after the primary. But although the approximately 7,000 black teenagers who turned 18 between the primary and general elections were a potential target group for additional registration efforts, the rest of the black population of Philadelphia appeared to be virtually totally registered (although some slack would become apparent as official list-cleansing continued). Apparently recognizing how few gains could be made from further registration efforts, Goode wisely decided to concentrate his resources in the general election campaign on reaching and bringing out to vote those of his supporters who were already registered.

Figured as a percentage of the voting-age population, black turnout was higher than white.

Turnout

Figured as a percentage of registered voters, the black and white turnout rates in the Democratic primary were almost the same: 68 percent for blacks and 70 percent for whites. But figured as a percentage of the voting-age population, black turnout was higher than white.

According to some sources, the turnout for Goode was due less to staff efforts than to the intense desire of blacks to come out and vote for Wilson Goode. Nobody brought them to the polls, and no-

> *Nobody brought [blacks] to the polls, and nobody had to bring them. They could not be kept away.*

body had to bring them. They could not be kept away.

Rizzo's staff had counted on an 85 percent turnout rate, but none of the wards carried by Rizzo reached that level. Polls had showed that Rizzo would lose to Goode, so some Rizzo supporters probably concluded that their votes would not matter.

The Republican primary race, in contrast, drew less than a 51 percent turnout rate of registered voters, even though the race was hotly contested by three viable, well-publicized candidates and the winner could anticipate a reasonable chance to do well in the general election no matter which Democrat won. Local political prognosticators thought that if Rizzo won, blacks would support a Republican in November, and that if Goode won, many white Democrats would vote Republican. (In fact, even though Goode won and many white Democrats did vote Republican in the general election, Goode's share of the white vote rose from 18 percent in the primary to 22.5 percent in the general election.)

In the actual primary voting, Goode's candidacy faced two problems. First, lack of voting experience on the part of many new voters cost him thousands of votes that went, instead, to Frank Lomento, a minor candidate who often enters local races. Lomento polled nearly 19,000 votes, most of them in black divisions. His name preceded Goode's on the machine, and the switch for his name was just before Goode's name. Apparently, many novice voters pulled this switch. Goode's margin of victory was more than adequate to cover the lost votes, but voter education efforts are needed to prevent such occurrences in the future.

Another problem concerned the long wait to vote. Rizzo people were outraged that even though the polls closed at 8 p.m., blacks were still voting at 10 and 11 p.m. that night. The reason is that the law allows all persons in line at the polling place by 8 p.m. to vote, and the lines were longer in black areas than in white areas—because of both the length of the ballot and the party preference of black voters. The ballot was very long and confusing—so much so that even experienced and sophisticated voters took much longer than usual, and some people took 8 to 10 minutes to mark their ballots. Long lines were therefore the rule of the day virtually everywhere. But for blacks the problem was compounded by the fact that they are overwhelmingly Democratic, and most polling places were assigned only two machines, one for Democrats and one shared by Republicans and the tiny Consumer party, which fielded a partial slate. In most white areas, a quarter of the voters or more used the second, or Republican, machine. But in black areas, where few voters were Republicans, the lines for the one usable Democratic machine built up until voters found themselves waiting hours to vote.

The early results on election night showed a close contest, since areas of Rizzo support were able to close the polls and tally results early. Surely many black voters in long lines at polling places, hearing of the closeness of the race or the early Rizzo lead, felt compelled to wait for a turn to vote. They waited—and that meant not only that previously unregistered blacks had registered and gone to the polls to vote, but, most importantly, that they would also endure some hardship to cast those votes. The reasons had to be a newfound sense of efficacy and the presence on the ballot of an electable candidate who genuinely inspired not only the black community but also some in the white community as well.

Previously unregistered blacks had registered and gone to the polls to vote, [and], most importantly, . . . they . . . also endure[d] some hardship to cast those votes.

List of Persons Interviewed

Lenore Berson, member, Wilson Goode campaign staff, and former chairperson, Philadelphia chapter of Americans for Democratic Action

John Furey, deputy commissioner of registration, City of Philadelphia

W. Wilson Goode, mayoral candidate in the Democratic primary

David Lewis, registration director, U.S. Bureau of the Census, Philadelphia

James McDonald, Election Bureau staff member, City of Philadelphia

Gregory Naylor, registration coordinator, 1983 primary campaign staff of Wilson Goode

Buddy Pitts, registration coordinator, 1983 primary campaign staff of Frank L. Rizzo

David Siegel, city planner and member, Philadelphia City Planning Commission

Fred Voigt, executive director, Committee of Seventy

Six additional interviewees—three Goode staffers, two Democratic ward leaders, and a Rizzo staffer—all wished to remain anonymous.

Endnotes

1. "Official nonpersonal voter registration application cards; preparation and distribution," *Purdon's Pennsylvania Statutes Annotated,* 1980. Title 623-19.1, added 1976, pp. 10, 11.

2. Of course, the census data may reflect an undercount of blacks. Or the black voting-age population may have grown after the 1980 census. However, although an additional 28,000 to 32,000 blacks did turn 18 between 1980 and April 1983 (when registration closed), the entry of that cohort into the voting-age population was probably offset by deaths. Moreover, between 1970 and 1980, outmigration caused a small but steady loss of blacks from the city (the total declined from 654,000 to 639,000), and that trend probably continued between 1980 and 1983 (U.S. Bureau of the Census, 1980 *Census of Population,* Volume 1, Chapter B; *General Population Characteristics,* Part 40, PC80-1-B40 [Washington, D.C.: Government Printing Office, 1982], pp. 40-123). But probably the most valid explanation for the high number of blacks registered in relation to the total black adult population is that there was a substantial number of duplicate registrations.

3. Sandra Featherman and William Rosenberg, *Jews, Blacks, and Ethnics: The "Vote White" Charter Campaign* (New York: American Jewish Committee, 1979).

4. The charter specifies that a person holding a position in city government must resign to run for any office other than the one he or she is currently holding. Incumbents, therefore, can run without penalty, but to run for a different office, a mayor, council member, or city employee must resign. The State Supreme Court has exempted the district attorney's office from this requirement on the grounds that that is a state office rather than a local one.

5. Twelve days before the election, the *Philadelphia Inquirer* stated: "Many politicians believe that the numbers of persons registered put out by the commissioner yesterday are high, and that the rolls include a significant number of duplicates. Those politicians note that the sheer magnitude of the registration influx—the office processed more than 250,000 forms—has made such duplication all but inevitable'' (May 5, 1983).

4. OVERCOMING THE POLITICS OF POLARIZATION IN BIRMINGHAM

Margaret K. Latimer and Robert S. Montjoy

Birmingham, Alabama, was made notorious in the first half of the 1960s by the fire hoses and police dogs of Bull Connor, commissioner of public safety, and by the bomb that killed four black girls in church. Since 1979, however, Birmingham's politics have been dominated by a black mayor. Elected in a close contest in 1979, Mayor Richard Arrington was reelected in October 1983 with 60 percent of the vote. His overwhelming reelection victory triumphantly demonstrated the success that black activists in Birmingham had achieved. For nearly a decade they had worked hard to increase black registration and political participation, to give the city's blacks greater electoral leverage and political power.

Sandwiched between Arrington's first and second victories were two elections in 1982 that helped mark the progress blacks were making as participants in the city's political life. One of the two 1982 elections was the Democratic primary contest for governor. Most of Birmingham's black community supported George McMillan, a resident of the city, in his race against former Governor George Wallace. Although McMillan received 64 percent of the vote in Jefferson County (Birmingham and its suburbs), he was forced into a run-off primary, which he lost by a statewide margin of 51.2 percent to 48.8 percent. Had a few more black votes been cast in Birmingham, the result might have been different.

The other of the two 1982 elections was the contest for the U.S. House of Representatives from Alabama's 6th district (most of metropolitan Birmingham—in other words, most of Jefferson County). Since 1964 the district had been repre-

[Mayor Richard Arrington's] overwhelming reelection victory triumphantly demonstrated the success that black activists in Birmingham had achieved.

sented by a Republican, but with strong black support the Democratic challenger, Ben Erdreich, defeated the one-term Republican incumbent, Albert Lee Smith, by a 54 percent to 46 percent margin.[1]

How had blacks managed to cover so much ground and reverse the course of history in less than two decades?

Background

In the 1950s and 1960s, civic affairs in Birmingham were dominated by the ultraconservative whites who backed Bull Connor as commissioner of public safety. And in the early 1960s, when blacks were attempting to register, the city's white establishment put up strong resistance.[2] In 1962, however, the city's commission form of government was changed to a mayor-council form, which meant that a single visible officer now represented the whole city and had control of patronage and services (including police department policies). In addition, the city council was enlarged from three members to nine, which meant that minority representation was more possible than before. Furthermore, in 1963 the voters elected a chief executive, Albert Boutwell, who was more moderate than his predecessors.

Today, when Birmingham's blacks speak of that period [of confrontation, harassment, and terror], they often refer to it as "the suffering of the 1960s."

But the year of Boutwell's election was also the year when Birmingham became a major focus of the nonviolent black protest movement led by the Reverend Martin Luther King, Jr. King's "Birmingham Manifesto," the street demonstrations that Bull Connor responded to with fire hoses and police dogs, and the church bombing all occurred in 1963; Governor Wallace stood in the schoolhouse door in Tuscaloosa to prevent school integration in 1964; in 1965, during the Selma march, a freedom rider was murdered. The atmosphere of confrontation between blacks and whites in Alabama had intensified, and black leaders were regularly being harassed and terrorized. Today, when Birmingham's blacks speak of that period, they often refer to it as "the suffering of the 1960s."

The state administration of then-segregationist Governor Wallace was so intransigent that black progress did not seem likely without outside intervention. That intervention came in the form of the Civil Rights Act of 1964 and the Voting Rights Act of 1965. With those federal actions, opportunities at once opened up for blacks across the South to register to vote. In 1960, black registration in Alabama was 13 percent of the eligible black voting-age population, but by 1970 it was 66 percent. In Birmingham, the city council that took office in 1968 appointed the first black person ever to sit on the council, Arthur Shores; a year later Shores was elected to the position.

In the meantime, a second barrier to black political representation in Alabama was also being lowered with the help of the federal government. Several reapportionment decisions in the federal courts, combined with enforcement of the Voting Rights Act, brought about a gradual lessening of racial gerrymandering. By the mid-1970s, blacks from Jefferson County had been elected to both houses of the state legislature.

But not all remnants of electoral discrimination disappeared immediately. In the 1970s the systems for electing members of the governing bodies of many city and county governments throughout the state were still inequitable.

In Birmingham, the nine-member city council is elected for four-year terms: five members are elected at each biennial election (in odd-numbered years), and the council member who has the lowest vote total in each election serves only a two-year term. But the five seats are undesignated and the vote is at-large—a system that generally tends to dilute a minority's vote.[3] Under that system, although 53 percent of Birmingham's registered voters are black[4] the majority of seats on the council were held by whites (until 1985, see page 79 below).[5]

On the Jefferson County Commission in the 1970s and early 1980s, the representation of blacks was also clearly not proportionate to their numbers. Three members were elected at-large for four-year terms, and although the county's population is one-

Countering the reluctance to get involved has been the strong organizational tradition of blacks in the South.

> *The real key to successful black registration efforts in Birmingham was the realization that blacks had had political success at the mayoral level.*

third black, all of the Jefferson County commissioners were white (until 1986).[6]

The long-standing inequity of black representation on the city council and the county commission probably contributed to political alienation and therefore indirectly depressed voter participation. Thus, neither black enfranchisement nor the integration of the public schools, which was under way at the same time, solved all the problems the black population faced in its attempt to achieve full civic equality. Election laws were still a major stumbling block to black participation.[7]

Moreover, the relative suddenness with which the black citizenry entered the electoral scene was a hindrance as well as a help. The novelty of having political power stimulated many blacks to participate, but many other blacks had a lingering reluctance to become involved. They might have been afraid, or they might have felt the apathy that some scholars argue is present among southern blacks.[8] Black leaders in Birmingham have expressed concern on both those counts. The state and regional black organizations refer to the fight against "apathy, an I-don't-care attitude."

Countering the reluctance to get involved has been the strong organizational tradition of blacks in the South. Scholars have found cooperative activity in support of group action to be more prevalent among southern blacks than among southern whites, even after socioeconomic factors are taken into account.[9] Certainly in Birmingham, a web of black organizational activity on behalf of political participation has been evident since the 1960s (see pages 70–71).

Another factor affecting the success of organizational efforts to increase black political participation has been the black community's perception of success at the polls. Scholars who have studied black politics in Mississippi have noted that "black electoral gains in various election situations, and the . . . perceptions" of those gains, may be important in increasing black participation.[10] The same idea was suggested to us by Simmie Lavender, former president of the Citizens Coalition (the most visible of the organizations in Birmingham that stress black voting, see page 71 below). He believes that the real key to successful black registration efforts in Birmingham was the realization that blacks had had political success at the mayoral level.

The Mayoral Elections of 1979 and 1983

In 1979, the Birmingham city government viewed black citizens much as Chicago's government did during the era of the Daley machine: "This black political participation was essentially a patron-client relationship where a few black 'leaders' delivered the black vote to their white patrons in exchange for a few political favors."[11] And police behavior was an issue in Birmingham, as it had been in Chicago in the 1970s, when blacks developed antagonism to the city's government.

In the mid-1970s, disenchanted with old-style politics, a group of Birmingham blacks broke away from the then-dominant Jefferson County Progressive Democratic Council and established the Citizens Coalition. Their efforts bore fruit in 1979, when a primary contest developed between incumbent Mayor David Vann and several city council members who were seeking his office. One of the latter was Richard Arrington.[12]

In a five-way race on October 7, Arrington got 44 percent of the vote, which surprised many Birmingham residents. Trying to explain his impressive total, the *Birmingham News* carried a map of black and white precincts and pointed to his solid support from the black community.[13] (Turnout by precinct for this election and for the run-off is included in Table 4-3, page 89.)

The run-off three weeks later pitted Arrington against conservative Councilman Frank Parsons. Arrington, who had the support of the incumbent mayor, received 51.1 percent of the vote; Parsons received 48.9 percent. Arrington defeated Parsons at the black polling places (precincts 38, 45, 43, 39, 44); Arrington also carried precinct 35, which the *News* considered biracial. The white polling places (precincts 34, 32, 40, 33) went to Parsons.

A labama's eligibility requirements are now about as liberal as those of most states and, according to reports by officials and activists, are not a significant barrier to registration.

Four years later, when Arrington ran for reelection in October 1983, most citizens of Birmingham were pleased with his administration, and black constituents took particular pride in his success. As the race between him and City Council President John Katopodis approached, black leaders intensified their effort to increase black registration and participation.

Both candidates said the issue was "leadership."[14] The city problems they discussed in the campaign had no bearing on race. Nevertheless, the vote was expected to divide along racial lines. Yet, even though the *Birmingham News* reported that Arrington's support in the white community was slight (an estimated 12 percent), both major city newspapers endorsed him and so did selected white business leaders, in a paid newspaper advertisement.

Richard Arrington was overwhelmingly reelected, receiving 60 percent of the vote. He estimated that he received 5-10 percent more of the vote in white areas than he had in 1979. In most areas, he also ran ahead of the two blacks who were incumbents on the city council (see page 78 below).[15]

The Legal Context

Electoral events are not the only context that is important to an analysis of the Jefferson County voter drives. One also needs to understand the legal context in which the drives have taken place. This includes—

- the legal requirements for registration;
- the application of the law by the board of registrars; and
- the voter re-identification program.

Legal Requirements for Registration. Although Alabama once had a number of restrictive criteria for registration and voting, the current legal requirements are rather simple. To qualify, a person must—

- be a citizen of the United States;
- be 18 years of age or older by the date of the election;

Citizens from many parts of the political spectrum have commented on the impressive performance of [Jefferson County's] Board of Registrars in making voter registration convenient and readily available.

- be a resident of the state and county in which registration is sought;
- not have been declared mentally incompetent; and
- not have been convicted of a disqualifying offense (such as a felony).

Alabama has no durational residence requirements. The requirements it used to have (one year in the state, six months in the county, three months in the ward or precinct) were declared unconstitutional in *Hadnot v. Amos*,[16] and no new regulations have been enacted. The result is that prospective voters may establish residence at any time up to the date at which the board of registrars cuts off registration for the coming election to prepare its records. (In Jefferson County, this cutoff date is 21 days before an election. Thus, all persons who arrive in Jefferson County at least 21 days before an election can register if they meet the requirements listed above.) Alabama's eligibility requirements are now about as liberal as those of most states and, according to reports by officials and activists, are not a significant barrier to registration.

Application of the Law. A second factor that may affect voter registration is the application of the law by a county's board of registrars. This varies significantly across Alabama's counties. In Jefferson County potential black voters find a reasonably open door. In fact, citizens from many parts of the political spectrum have commented on the impressive performance of the county's board of registrars in making voter registration convenient and readily available.

The legal situation in Jefferson County is quite different from the legal situation in most other Alabama counties. Because of its size, Jefferson was exempted in many respects from the general act governing registrars and was allowed to operate under a local act (an act of the legislature that applies to only one county or a few counties in a specified population range). All other boards of registrars in Alabama consist of three political appointees whose four-year terms coincide with those of the appointing state officials. Most boards have no staff. The

Jefferson County . . . has a number of black deputy registrars, whereas many other counties and some large cities [in Alabama] have none.

***B**lack registration activity in Jefferson County is a constant low-profile effort in which many overlapping organizations and individuals take part.*

Jefferson County board consists of one person whose term does not rotate and who has a staff of county merit-system employees. This arrangement has, in effect, provided the county with more professionalism, longevity, and expertise than is the norm across the state.

The importance of this is easy to overlook because statutes and court decisions have made the processing of applications for registration a virtually uniform, ministerial function throughout the state. But boards retain considerable discretion with regard to their accessibility to applicants. Although state law establishes the number of session days (the number of days that the board can be paid for working) for each county and specifies a few out-of-session days (such as one at each four-year college in the county), the choice of when to schedule these days—in most counties, somewhere between 120 and 168 days per year—is left to the board. Until recently, the law also permitted but did not require the boards to appoint deputy registrars—volunteers who could work as many days as they wished and take applications anywhere in the county. (Recent legislation requires the appointment of deputy registrars.) Thus, in the most restrictive counties, prospective registrants had to apply in person before the board, usually at the courthouse, on one of the appointed session days, the bulk of which might or might not coincide with a registration drive. In Jefferson County, the registration office in the courthouse is open full time, five days a week from 8 a.m. to 5 p.m., throughout the year.

Moreover, although in the past some boards in Alabama refused to appoint deputy registrars, the Jefferson County board was not one of them. In fact, Jefferson County has far more deputy registrars than most of Alabama's counties. Jefferson County also has a number of black deputy registrars, whereas many other counties and some large cities have none.[17] (Black leaders in Birmingham attribute their success in getting black registrars to the political power that blacks have developed within the city and county, and they especially attribute their success to pressure from the black members of Jefferson County's delegation to the state legislature.)

Deputy registrars in Jefferson County are given instructions at the office of the board of registrars and take an oath before serving. All public librarians in the city of Birmingham are deputy registrars. City clerks in municipalities within Jefferson County are also deputy registrars. In addition, the League of Women Voters in Birmingham, although not a predominantly black organization, has long been interested in voter registration, especially at black high schools. According to E. J. Stephens, president of the Birmingham chapter of the league in the mid-1980s, roughly 20 members of the organization were deputized as registrars and served in special places and on specific occasions as sanctioned by the board of registrars. (Black leaders speak approvingly of the work of the Birmingham chapter of the league.) All clerks who work for the board of registrars are also deputized, and they frequently serve at various city locations when neighborhood leaders request deputy registrars.

In discussing black registration in Birmingham, most black leaders immediately mention Ornie McAlpin, a black deputy registrar who has worked full time as a volunteer for the official Jefferson County Board of Registrars. McAlpin, a retired high school guidance counselor, goes about the community meeting people and presenting voter education information—and many of the people she talks to become registered voters. Numerous observers say that she personally oversees and coordinates much of the black registration in Birmingham.

Voter Re-identification Program. In Alabama, voter registration is permanent. Registrants remain on the rolls, regardless of their voting history, until the board of registrars receives information that they have died, established residence elsewhere, been declared mentally incompetent, or been convicted of a disqualifying offense. Of course, such information does not always come to the board; as a result, the registration rolls in many Alabama counties are inflated. In 1980, for example, in 12 counties the number of registered voters was higher than the voting-age population.

[The] traditional black groups have been joined by numerous other black organizations in a loosely coordinated but complementary effort to increase black electoral leverage.

To deal with this problem, a number of counties, including Jefferson, have conducted re-identification programs, each of which has been authorized by separate local legislation. A Jefferson County program began in the spring of 1981. Voters were notified of the re-identification requirement by notices published in the city's several newspapers and mailed with tax bills and auto tags. Voters could re-identify by returning a short form that was mailed with the notices or by going to the office of the board, in the courthouse. After March 1982, the names of persons who had not re-identified were taken off the active registration list. From that date on, individuals could re-identify only by going to the courthouse in person. Former registrants could re-identify as late as election day if they went to the courthouse and obtained a certificate permitting them to vote.

The re-identification program may have had a negative impact on registration. All voters had to take some action to keep their names on the rolls, and people with a marginal involvement in politics would be least likely to do so.

Organizational Dynamics

According to Grover Smith, NAACP field director in the early 1980s, black registration activity in Jefferson County is a constant low-profile effort in which many overlapping organizations and individuals take part.

The Citizens Coalition, which Richard Arrington was instrumental in organizing in the mid-1970s and which today is the most active political group in Birmingham, . . . is a network of people who favor energetic black political activity.

The NAACP was the mainstay of nonpartisan registration and voter participation activity in Birmingham and Jefferson County during the 1970s and early 1980s.[18] It provided a relatively stable organizational foundation as well as monetary support. Today, it operates several branches within the city, rather than a central office. The Southern Christian Leadership Conference (SCLC), which was founded in Birmingham in 1954, also has consistently been a potent force. And since the late 1960s the Alabama Democratic Conference (the black arm of the state Democratic party) has magnified the political power of the black population statewide, even though it is not of major importance within the city of Birmingham. It has given priority to, and achieved its greatest successes with, court cases on reapportionment throughout the state.[19]

Those traditional black groups have been joined by numerous other black organizations in a loosely coordinated but complementary effort to increase black electoral leverage. The work of the A. Philip Randolph Institute both parallels and reflects the black political activities of the biracial Birmingham Labor Council. The interdenominational Clergy That Care has made voter registration one of its priorities. And black civic groups such as the Hungry Club also support black political participation.

Candidate-oriented organizations, many of which are biracial, also stress black voting activity. The strongest of these is the Citizens Coalition, which Richard Arrington was instrumental in organizing in the mid-1970s and which today is the most active political group in Birmingham. The coalition is a network of people who favor energetic black political activity; at the time of its founding it was a spin-off from a less aggressive "wait-and-see" black organization, the Jefferson County Progressive Democratic Council, that some people had termed "elitist." The Citizens Coalition, which has an open membership policy, aims to be a grassroots organization and seeks to eradicate the residue of black fear generated in the past by authoritarian city governments. Members of the coalition are active in educational and civic groups, where they monitor city activities and encourage blacks to participate in politics. Although the organization clearly supports Richard Arrington, it does not associate itself with a political party (for example, the group endorsed Republican Congressman John Buchanon in the 1970s). In contrast, the Jefferson County Progressive Democratic Council is part of the state Democratic party.

Since most black political communication in Birmingham is by word of mouth, gatherings of citizens are crucial in creating the necessary links. Until the NAACP phased out its state field direc-

Since most black political communication in Birmingham is by word of mouth, gatherings of citizens are crucial in creating the necessary links.

The neighborhood and community associations that are a significant part of the organizational structure supporting black political participation stem from federal directives for urban development.

tors, its office in downtown Birmingham appeared to be the primary meeting, working, and organizing place for black volunteer workers from many different groups. Neighborhood and community associations and black churches provide other contact points where activists have been able to meet the people of Birmingham and the rest of Jefferson County.

Interestingly, the neighborhood and community associations that are a significant part of the organizational structure supporting black political participation stem from federal directives for urban development. In 1974, Birmingham was divided into 22 "neighborhoods," which were then subdivided into 93 "communities" to qualify for federal community development block grant funds. (The Birmingham plan is considered a model in its emphasis on citizen input into urban planning.) Both the designated neighborhoods and the communities have presidents, vice presidents, and secretaries, who are charged with communicating to the mayor's office their own areas' needs for development funds. The neighborhoods have block captains reminiscent of those in the well-organized city regimes of the past century.

This framework of neighborhood associations has supported both nonpolitical and political activities. Nonpolitically, members of the neighborhood associations help their neighbors in various ways—for example, by demonstrating an interest in youth activities, by working for urban beautification, or by forming "watch groups" to facilitate police protection and prevent crime. Politically, the neighborhood associations have been useful as centers of communication for political activity and as ladders and training grounds for black political activists. Two of the 1983 challengers for seats on the city council, for example, were presidents of neighborhood associations, as were two of the successful black candidates for the council in 1985. Simmie Lavender, for many years the president of Citizens Coalition, was and still is a neighborhood president.

Because the neighborhoods concentrate on general civic good, they have staying power between elections. Their civic concerns are the glue holding them together. And when they do become actively involved in politics, their appeals are less strident than might be the case if they were not associated with a network of neighborhood activities.

Black churches, which have been central to black political activity since the inception of the civil rights movement, are the other main part of the organizational structure. Many blacks learned the techniques of organizing and administering from their involvement with the church; religious and political activities frequently overlap; and some of the more prominent black ministers in Birmingham serve as leaders in the area of social and civic concerns as well as in politics. For example, the Reverend Abraham Woods and the Reverend Nelson Smith of the SCLC have been activists within Birmingham's black community since the 1950s; the Reverend John Porter was once an assistant to the Reverend Martin Luther King, Jr., at the latter's church in Montgomery; the Reverend E. W. Jarrett is a member of Mayor Arrington's advisory committee and serves as chairman of Clergy That Care; and two black pastors have served in the Alabama legislature. Summing up the involvement of the black clergy in Birmingham's black politics, Bishop Phillip Cousin of the AME Church commented, "Ethics must be a part of your total religious commitment. What I am civicly, politically, economically, socially—all are a result of what I am theologically."[20]

Outreach Activities

Because the voter participation drives in Birmingham have been part of a neighborhood-related and/or religious movement rather than a bureaucratic effort, the organizations involved have not kept accurate enough records of their activities for us to prepare a detailed description. What has emerged from conversations with black leaders is a general picture of the methods used to promote registration and turnout.

Because the neighborhoods concentrate on general civic good, they have staying power between elections.

73

Registration

Leaders of civic groups encourage neighborhood leaders in low-participation areas to request deputy registrars from the county board of registrars. At that point a special registration drive goes into effect in the neighborhood, perhaps at a school or a shopping center. The registrars who serve in the neighborhoods frequently keep later hours than the board of registrars.

Both the young and the old are specially targeted for registration. Registration organizers sometimes use sound trucks playing rock music to gain the attention of the young, particularly those just turning 18. Girl Scouts, Boy Scouts, and Metropolitan Crusaders (members of a teenage civic group) help distribute leaflets explaining the importance of political participation. And registration services may also be offered at county nutrition centers frequented by the elderly. Since many of the elderly lived through the turbulent era when black participation either was an ordeal or put them at economic risk, organizers have more to overcome than simple apathy.

During the early 1980s at the NAACP office, volunteers worked from city directories and registration lists to identify unregistered citizens. Low-income neighborhoods and housing projects were frequently targeted for registration. Personal contact, printed handouts, or "tags" placed on the front doors of the unregistered were used to encourage political activity. Workers themselves were encouraged with awards and were sometimes paid stipends. According to then-NAACP Field Director Smith, the NAACP paid partial expenses for roughly eight volunteer black deputy registrars. A stipend of $75 per month was the usual expenditure to promote such volunteer activity.

Black churches . . . have been central to black political activity since the inception of the civil rights movement.

The SCLC has provided a different kind of encouragement to citizens. The Reverend Abraham Woods, head of the Birmingham chapter, uses emotional concerns to arouse sympathy and generate energy among the public—a sympathy and energy that can then be redirected to political participation. For example, the Reverend Woods repeatedly refers to the accidental death of a black woman during a police chase in the early 1980s: that tragedy helped him motivate blacks to become active citizens.

The SCLC conducts workshops and mass meetings to encourage registration. Its rallies combine entertainment and refreshments with instructions on filling out registration forms. Since the SCLC is especially aware of the importance of the media in communicating with the black population, it enlists popular radio disc jockeys to publicize its voter education activities.

Turnout

Long-term efforts are continually directed at black voter registration. Then at election time, short-term efforts are directed at getting out the vote (GOTV). Like registration efforts, GOTV drives have been advanced primarily by nonpartisan black civic groups such as the NAACP, although the campaign organizations of candidates running for office at the state and national levels have also been greatly concerned with getting voters to the polls. In Birmingham, the Citizens Coalition is the organization with the greatest outreach.

Shortly before an election, the groups put certain standard election routines into operation. The NAACP provides local ministers with "election day sermons." Volunteers distribute leaflets produced at the national level of the NAACP, linking welfare, unemployment, and hunger to the need to vote. Various groups publish ads in city newspapers offering voters transportation to the polls. On election day, buses borrowed from local churches transport voters. In 1982, the NAACP spent roughly $3,500 on gasoline for buses, food for bus drivers, and stipends for workers.

Between 1979 and the present, the elections to which those activities have been particularly applied are not only Richard Arrington's race for mayor in 1979 (discussed above on page 65), but also—

- the 1982 governor's race;
- the 1982 congressional race in the 6th district;
- Arrington's 1983 race for reelection as mayor; and
- the 1983 and 1985 city council races.

Both the young and the old are specially targeted for registration.

Like registration efforts, GOTV drives have been advanced primarily by nonpartisan black civic groups such as the NAACP.

The 1982 Gubernatorial Election. All candidates for governor in 1982 solicited black votes in Birmingham. The Birmingham-based Democratic candidate, George McMillan, had substantial local black support, and black groups enthusiastically promoted turnout in both of the Democratic gubernatorial primaries (the first round and the run-off). After McMillan lost to George Wallace in the run-off, the Alabama Democratic Conference endorsed Wallace against conservative Republican Emory Folmar in the general election. With the help of black votes, Wallace went on to win.

The 1982 Congressional Election. Blacks in Birmingham and the rest of Jefferson County were also heavily involved in the congressional race for the 6th district in 1982. Indeed, it is hard to tell which of the two races—the gubernatorial or the congressional—was more important in promoting turnout.

Blacks were considered "natural constituents" of the Democratic congressional nominee, Ben Erdreich. The Alabama Democratic Conference endorsed him, and most leaders of black organizations in Birmingham vigorously favored his candidacy. His opponent, incumbent Republican Albert Lee Smith, was a conservative with ties to the Moral Majority.

The 6th district in 1982 was not the same as it had been in 1980 when Congressman Smith was first elected. After the census of 1980, the district's boundaries were enlarged by the addition of the two Jefferson County communities of Brighton and Roosevelt City. Both are heavily populated by unionized, mostly black, blue-collar workers. This group was considered crucial to the Erdreich campaign.

The biracial Birmingham Labor Council was especially instrumental in increasing the participation of blacks on behalf of Erdreich. The council put significant monetary resources into the A. Philip Randolph Institute, an allied and nationally-oriented political group. The institute, in turn, generated voting support for Erdreich within the black community.

The Erdreich campaign took part in a statewide Democratic get-out-the-vote effort, which included a telethon, telephone banks, and neighborhood canvasses.[21]

The 1983 Mayoral Election. The mayoral race in October 1983 was another occasion for the loose, yet well coordinated, electoral network to go into action within Birmingham's black community.

Various groups and individuals were assigned responsibility for getting out the vote in specific neighborhoods. In the days leading up to the election, volunteers of all ages, including college and high school students, went from door to door urging political participation. Sample ballots were distributed in person, many in black churches. A centralized phone bank, handled mostly by volunteers, was in touch with all segments of the community. Cindy McCartney, a professional political consultant who had helped Arrington in 1979, returned to Birmingham in 1983 to guide both the phone bank and a program of direct-mail communications.[22] Although some television advertising was used and prominent members of the clergy (such as the Reverend Abraham Woods) produced radio tapes that were aired at all times of the day, most of the voter contact was personalized.

Information on voters, even down to the block level, was a major part of the effort. The mayor's office had citywide lists of registrants, and the NAACP had developed lists of registrants for each polling place. Targeting election districts that had high percentages of black registrants, Arrington's campaign staff gave area leaders the names and addresses of the registrants for whom they were to be responsible, and block captains used those lists to locate voters.

On the Saturday before the election, organizational leaders met with black ministers at a brunch to plan the pre-election activities. Ministers were asked to lend buses to transport voters to the polls. (NAACP support included financial backing for gasoline and the expenses of the drivers; the NAACP spent $1,800 on this GOTV effort.) On Sunday, ser-

In assessing the success of [Mayor Arrington's reelection] campaign, community political leaders felt that the key elements in the mayor's large victory were the careful organizing of block captains and the telephone bank operation.

mons on the election were delivered from most black pulpits. On Monday, voter rallies were held, as were the all-important organizational meetings of the roughly 1,600 block leaders who would be responsible for getting out the vote. On Tuesday—election day—buses circled around black precincts to make transportation available and convenient. In an effort to turn out every possible black vote, groups used record-keeping methods similar to those devised by campaign management firms. Block captains, monitoring voting throughout the day, compared turnout to registration lists and attempted to contact the people who had not voted.

Arrington received 60 percent of the city's vote. Afterward, in assessing the success of the campaign, community political leaders felt that the key elements in the mayor's large victory were the careful organizing of block captains and the telephone bank operation. No doubt an additional special ingredient was the enthusiastic effort by all levels of leadership.

The 1983 and 1985 City Council Elections. In the 1983 and 1985 campaigns for seats on the city council, much the same kind of effort took place. Sample ballots were distributed, meetings were held in churches, and telephone banks were used.

Five city council seats were up for election in 1983. Two years before, in 1981, the Citizens Coalition had endorsed a slate of five black candidates for council seats—and was criticized for being preoccupied with race. This time, from among 18 candidates for the council, the Citizens Coalition endorsed two white incumbents, two black incumbents, and two black challengers. Other groups, including one representing the white community, also chose biracial slates—a move forward for race relations in Birmingham. (Among the candidates endorsed by the white group were the two black incumbents.)

Four of the incumbent council members (the two blacks and two of the whites) were reelected. The only council incumbent who was defeated was white, and the two black challengers whom the Citi-

Between 1971 and 1981, 36,421 new black registrants were added to the rolls—an increase of 57 percent over the 1971 base.

zens Coalition had endorsed ended up in a run-off for his seat. Thus, four of the six candidates endorsed by the coalition had received clear majorities, and the run-off between the other two endorsed blacks added a third black to the nine-member council.

The city council election in 1985 was an even greater victory for the Citizens Coalition. The sample ballots circulated by the coalition endorsed five candidates: one black incumbent, one white incumbent, and three other black candidates. In the October 7 election, four of those candidates were elected outright, and one (Andris Hinton, the black mayor of Brownville) went into a run-off against an incumbent (Bettye Fine Collins). Although Hinton had the coalition's backing, Collins won with 53 percent of the vote.

The *Birmingham News* noted that in the run-off, turnout increased in white precincts and decreased in black precincts. Race was not an issue in the contest, the *News* reported on October 27, but it was certainly an "important cue."

Thus, even though the coalition fell short of a perfect score in 1985, the election produced a council where blacks constituted a majority for the first time.

The most dramatic increases in registration followed rather than preceded the 1979 election of Richard Arrington.

Effectiveness

To assess the specific impact of black mobilization efforts, we collected and analyzed the data on voter registration and voter turnout that we received from the Jefferson County Board of Registrars in July 1983 and from the city clerk of Birmingham in both July and October 1983.[23] Data on registration were by race, but data on turnout by race were unavailable. We do, however, have estimates of turnout in majority-black areas.*

---

*We thank Beverly Williams, formerly a member of the staff of the Auburn University Office of Public Service and Research, for her many hours of data preparation and for creating the computer data set.

In 1978, in 10 of the 15 precincts whites had a higher registration rate than blacks. By 1982, however, ... in 10 of the precincts blacks had a higher registration rate than whites.

The population data for precincts in Jefferson County were aggregated from the Census data issued to the state of Alabama to enable the state to prepare its 1982 reapportionment plans. Those data represent the earliest version of the 1980 census.[24]

The **registration** percentage, or "registration rate," as we shall call it for convenience, is derived by dividing the number of registered voters of a race by the voting-age population of that race. **Turnout** we report as the percentage *of the voting-age population* that casts ballots, *not* the percentage of registered voters. Many reporters and politicians have the habit of reporting voter turnout as the percentage of registered voters, but that greatly inflates the public's perception of the number of citizens who vote. Moreover, because registration rates vary greatly, that habit introduces a major source of error into the comparisons of participation rates. Therefore, we consider it unwise to report voter turnout as the percentage of registered voters except when data on the voting-age population are unavailable.[25]

Registration

Were the black registration drives in Jefferson County successful? To answer this question affirmatively, we must—

- show that black registration increased, and
- rule out plausible explanations other than the registration drives.

The first task is quite simple. After a voter re-identification in 1971, black registration rose from 63,379 in 1972 to 99,800 in 1981. In other words, between 1971 and 1981, 36,421 new black registrants were added to the rolls—an increase of 57 percent over the 1971 base.

What are the probable causes of that gain?

An increase in population explains part of the increase in registration. The number of voting-age blacks rose from 123,091 in 1970 to 149,172 in 1980. But we can control for population growth by calculating registration as a percentage of voting-age population. (We estimated black voting-age population over time by a linear interpolation of Census data between 1970 and 1980 and by extrapolation beyond 1980.)

The results of our calculation appear in Figure 4-1. Between 1972 and 1976, the registration rate was essentially flat: blacks were registering, but the increase only kept up with the estimated increase in population. Then from 1976 through 1981 the rate of registration rose impressively, going from 50 percent to 66 percent. During that five-year period, registration increased much more rapidly than population.

Figure 4-1
Black Registration as a Percentage of Voting-Age Population, Jefferson County, 1972–1981

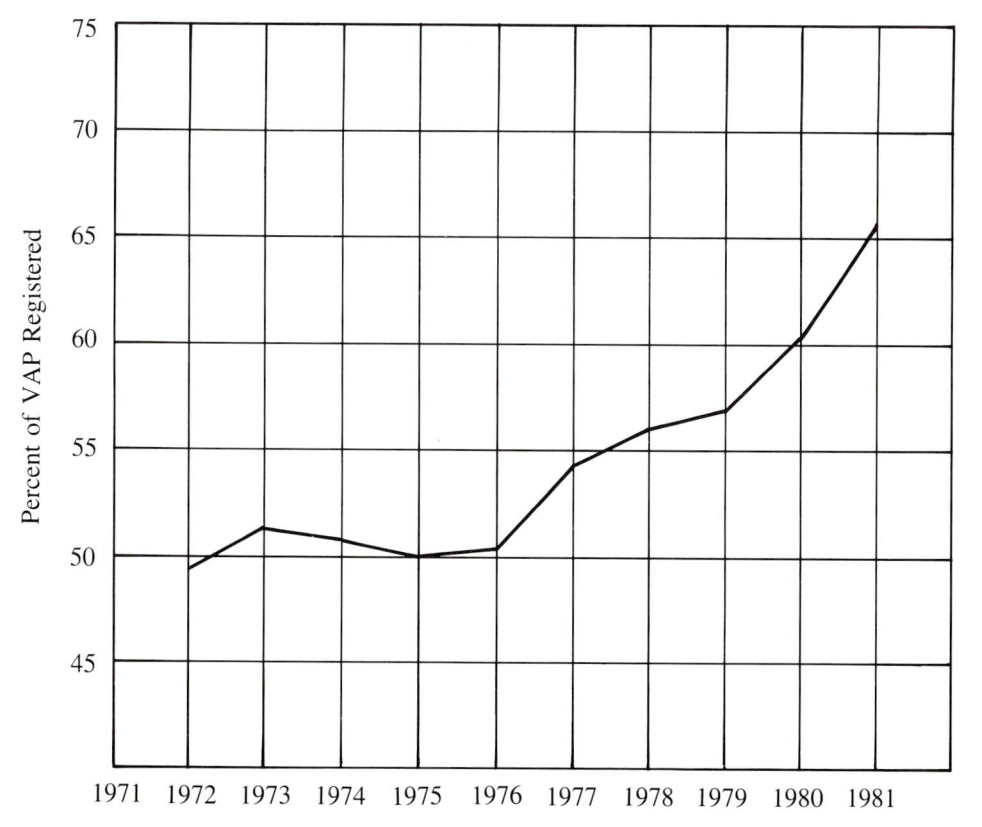

Another possible explanation for the increase in registration is roll inflation. The more distant the date of the previous re-identification of voters, the greater the build-up of names of people who have died or moved away. Some roll inflation is evidenced by the fact that after a re-identification in 1982, the number of registered blacks dropped from 99,000 to 86,890, or from 66 percent to 56 percent of the estimated voting-age population. The loss may be partly due to the failure of some current residents to re-identify.

But even if the entire drop were attributable to roll inflation, the registration rate would still have increased 7 percentage points between 1972 and 1982. (That was no small accomplishment, because the new registrants had to be drawn from the ranks of groups that tend to have low participation rates: new arrivals, people who have just reached voting age, and older residents who have not responded to previous registration efforts.)

Thus, neither population growth nor roll inflation can account for all or even most of the increase in black voter registration. We are left to conclude that organized efforts were largely responsible. That conclusion is borne out by the timing of the increase. The black leaders we interviewed agreed that concern about black political participation intensified in the mid-1970s, when the Citizens Coalition was formed—and as Figure 4-1 shows, that was the period during which black registration rates rose. (Interestingly, the most dramatic increases in registration followed rather than preceded the 1979 election of Richard Arrington. We will discuss this point in greater detail below.)

Between 1978 and 1982, the relationship between black and white registration rates in Jefferson County as a whole reversed itself.

Black Registration at the Precinct Level. For a more detailed picture, Table 4-1 lists changes in black and white registration rates by precinct during the intervals 1978-80 and 1980-82. During the first interval, registration activity was under no re-identification constraints; the second interval covers a period of re-identification (see page 70 above for a description of the re-identification process). For reference, Table 4-1 gives the black percentage of each

Table 4-1
Changes in Registration Percentages as a Proportion of Voting-Age Population, by Precinct, 1978–1982 (Jefferson County)

Precinct	% Black Pop.	Change 1978–1980 (Before Re-ident.) Black (%)	Change 1978–1980 (Before Re-ident.) White (%)	Change 1980–1982 (After Re-ident.) Black (%)	Change 1980–1982 (After Re-ident.) White (%)
34	1	n.a.*	+ 3	n.a.	− 10
51	2	+ 14	− 9	− 1	− 19
15	3	+ 12	+ 13	+ 2	− 7
31	4	+ 5	+ 9	0	− 16
35	4	n.a.	+ 9	n.a.	− 7
50	6	n.a.	+ 8	n.a.	− 10
49	8	n.a.	− 2	n.a.	0
14	9	+ 2	+ 8	− 4	− 4
32	9	+ 17	+ 8	+ 15	− 17
42	11	n.a.	+ 9	n.a.	− 11
52	12	+ 4	+ 3	− 9	− 4
40	22	+ 17	0	+ 18	− 12
33	35	+ 2	+ 19	+ 3	− 12
36	39	+ 4	+ 7	+ 1	− 11
37	62	+ 4	n.a.	− 12	n.a.
41	62	+ 4	+ 9	− 10	− 15
38	66	+ 5	− 5	+ 6	− 21
45	68	+ 4	− 1	0	− 1
43	70	+ 7	− 2	− 6	− 6
39	75	+ 5	− 2	− 6	− 11
44	80	+ 5	− 2	− 8	− 6
Average Change		+ 6.9	+ 4.0	− 0.7	− 11.1

*Not available, see Note 24.

precinct's population, and the precincts are arranged in ascending order of that percentage.

Between 1978 and 1980, all precincts showed growth in black registration rates, and in four of the precincts the growth was higher than 10 percent. The average growth per precinct in black registration as a percentage of voting-age population was 6.9 percent. (The average growth in white registration was 4 percent.)

During the second interval, the black registration rate increased in six precincts, remained constant in two, and declined in eight, for an average decrease of only 0.7 percent. Since all voters were required to re-identify, apparently black organizational activity offset the losses in black registration caused by purging after the re-identification. (The white registration rate dropped in every precinct but one, where it remained constant, for an average decrease of 11.1 percent.)

> *Apparently, . . . black turnout does not grow as fast as black registration.*

Differences in Black and White Registration Levels. Historically, registration rates for the black population in Jefferson County and in Birmingham have been lower than comparable rates for the white population. Therefore, we tabulated the differences in registration rates between blacks and whites in 15 of the county's precincts for three election years (1978, 1980, and 1982; see Table 4-2). In the county's other 6 precincts—5 predominantly white and 1 predominantly black—data were lacking (see note 24). The designations W (white) and B (black) on the table indicate a comparative advantage (in percentage points) for the white or black race, respectively.

In 1978, in 10 of the 15 precincts whites had a higher registration rate than blacks. By 1982, however, the historical pattern had been reversed: in 10 of the precincts blacks had a higher registration rate than whites. In 1982 in 3 of the other 5 precincts (31, 14, 36), the registration rate for whites was more than 20 percentage points higher than for blacks, and in the remaining 2 precincts (51, 41) whites had an advantage, but a smaller one. Even in the precincts where whites were heavily registered, however, between 1980 and 1982 the differences between white and black registration rates decreased. A large part of the apparent decrease must be attributed to the purging of voter rolls by re-identification.[26]

The industriousness of Birmingham's black leaders in organizing black registration drives seems especially striking when one compares a majority-black precinct that lies outside the city (precinct 41) with the five majority-black precincts inside the city

Table 4-2
Differences Between Black and White Registration Percentages as a Proportion of Black and White Voting-Age Populations, Respectively, by Precinct, 1978–1982 (Jefferson County)

Precinct	% Black Pop.	1978 (%)	1980 (%)	1982 (%)
		Differences in Registration Rates		
34‡	1	n.a.*	na.	n.a.
51	2	23W†	20W	2W
15	3	5W	6W	4B†
31	4	68W	72W	56W
35	4	n.a.	n.a.	n.a.
50	6	n.a.	n.a.	n.a.
49	8	n.a.	n.a.	n.a.
14	9	28W	27W	27W
32‡	9	38W	29W	3B
42	11	n.a.	n.a.	n.a.
52	12	14B	15B	10B
40‡	22	16W	1B	31B
33‡	35	28W	11W	4B
36	39	41W	44W	32W
37	62	n.a.	n.a.	n.a.
41	62	29W	34W	17W
38‡	66	4W	10B	37B
45‡	68	41B	46B	49B
43‡	70	34B	43B	43B
39‡	75	25B	32B	37B
44‡	80	23B	20B	36B
Mean Difference		9.5W	5.1W	8.0B

*Not available, see Note 24.
†"B" indicates that the black registration rate exceeds the white registration rate by the amount given, and "W" indicates that the white registration rate exceeds the black registration rate by the amount given.
‡Precincts within the city of Birmingham.

(38, 45, 43, 39, 44). In precinct 41, in 1982 the white registration rate was still 17 percentage points higher than the black rate.[27] But in four of the five majority-black precincts within Birmingham, in 1982 black registration rates outdistanced white rates by an amazing 36 percentage points or more. This suggests that white participation in those precincts was dampened by whites' discomfort with their minority status.

Between 1978 and 1982, the relationship between black and white registration rates in Jefferson County as a whole reversed itself. In 1978, the white registration rate in the county was 9.5 percentage points above the black rate. Within four years, the black rate was 8.0 percentage points above the white rate.

A white backlash against black registration efforts was always a possibility. But in the areas within the city of Birmingham—where competition between white and black voters for political control is heavier than it is elsewhere—white registration during the 1978-80 period increased less than it did in areas that lie largely outside the city (Table 4-1). In the nine precincts within the city (34, 32, 40, 33, 38, 45, 43, 39, 44) the average increase in the white registration rate was 2 percent; in the precincts outside the city, the average increase in the white rate was 4.7 percent. Thus, backlash in the form of white counter-registration was probably not involved. (During periods of re-identification—in other words, the period 1980-82—one cannot measure change accurately enough to comment on backlash.)

Turnout

In Jefferson County total turnout has been on the rise, although for many years it was well below the national average. Between 1978 and 1982 the average increase countywide was 12 percent (from a mean of 26 percent to a mean of 38 percent of the voting-age population). For the presidential election of 1980, the mean turnout in the county was 46 percent. For the election of 1986, the mean turnout in the county was 46.7 percent—more than 4 points above the state average and more than 9 points above the national average. (Turnout in Birmingham and other metropolitan areas in Alabama has usually lagged behind turnout in other parts of the state.)

Turnout in most of the county's heavily black precincts has usually been slightly below the county average. Apparently, therefore, black turnout does not grow as fast as black registration. Organizational efforts to get black voters to the polls are probably

Although blacks were registering by 1982, they might not have been voting as heavily as whites.

more restrained, for several reasons. First, GOTV drives are significantly more expensive than registration drives. Second, GOTV drives, according to the NAACP's Grover Smith, require more intensive efforts. Finally, recognizing that members of the electorate have the right to their personal decisions on whether to vote, organizational leaders may feel it less appropriate to push people to turn out on election day than to coax them into the routine act of registering.

Black organizations in Birmingham target specific neighborhoods in the city's five majority-black precincts for voter mobilization efforts. Nevertheless, in statewide elections, voter turnout is consistently lower in the majority-black city than in the the county as a whole. For example, in the general election of 1978 the city had a 21 percent turnout rate, whereas the county had a 26 percent turnout rate; in the general election of 1982, the city's rate was 31 percent and the county's was 38 percent. However, parts of Jefferson County include the highest-income districts in the state of Alabama, and high socioeconomic status generally means high turnout. Such precincts inflate the county's turnout average. (In the 1980 general election, turnout in the high-income districts of the county was between 68 and 74 percent of the voting-age population.)

Figure 4-2 is a scattergram relating precinct turnout in Jefferson County in the 1982 general election to the percentage of each precinct's population that is black. In the four precincts where turnout was higher than 50 percent, the black population is very low. The slope of the line downward as black population increases indicates that the higher the black percentage, the lower the turnout (slope of regression line = −.20). This suggests that although blacks were registering by 1982, they might not have been voting as heavily as whites.

The 1979 and 1983 Mayoral Elections. Within Birmingham itself, black turnout drives have been more vigorous and thus more successful than in the county at large, especially in mayoral elections. (See Table 4-3 for turnout by precinct in selected elections from 1978 to 1983.)

The [white] turnout figures (as opposed to the registration figures) suggest something akin to backlash.

Figure 4-2
Turnout in Relation to Black Percentage of Population, by Precinct, Jefferson County, 1982 General Election

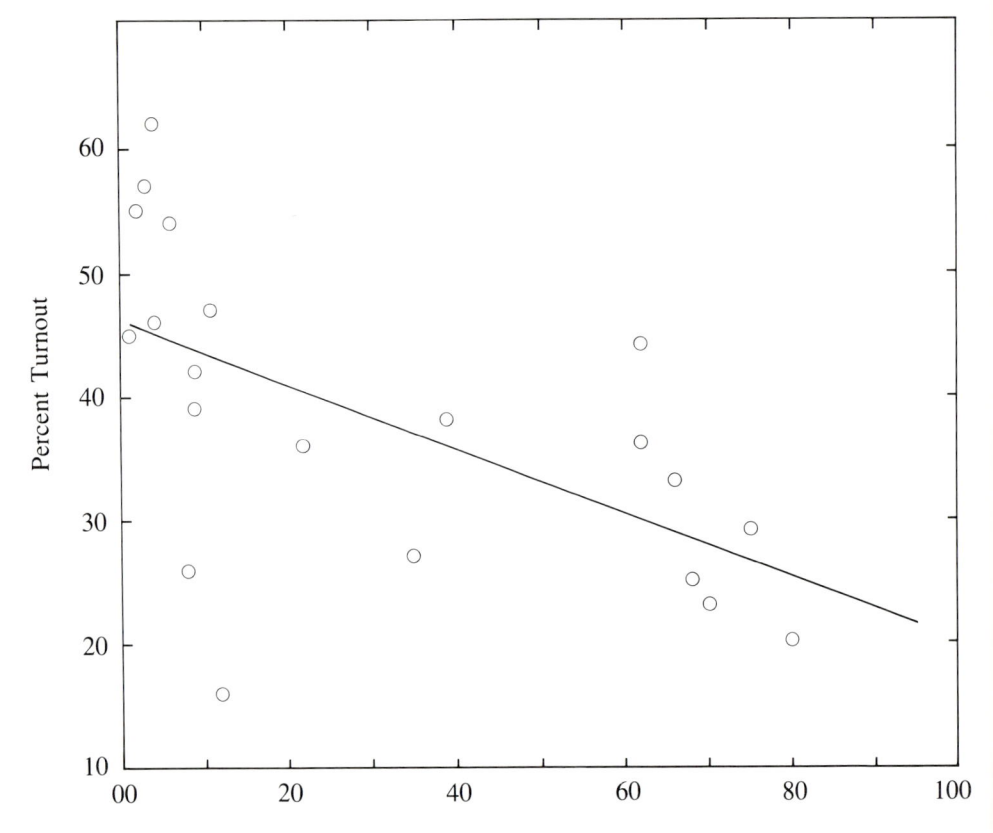

In the 1979 run-off between Arrington and Parsons, turnout was heavy. The *News* reported that "68 percent of the electorate" voted.[28] Black turnout in the primary had not been large, but turnout in the majority-black precincts increased by 4.2 percentage points between the primary and the run-off. Arrington's impressive showing in the first round apparently reinforced the confidence of black citizens in their political potential. For example, according to the *News*, turnout at the Wenonah Junior

Table 4-3
Turnout as a Percentage of Voting-Age Population in Birmingham Precincts, 1978–1982

Precinct	% Black Pop.	1978 Governor/Congress Primary (%)	1978 Run-Off (%)	1978 General (%)	1979 Mayor Primary (%)	1979 Mayor Run-Off (%)	1980 President/Congress Primary (%)	1980 Run-Off (%)	1980 General (%)	1982 Governor/Congress Primary (%)	1982 Run-Off (%)	1982 General (%)	1983 Mayor Primary (%)
White													
34	1	28	35	37	37	48	21	6	59	35	33	45	44
32	9	24	29	32	31	37	21	6	54	28	30	42	38
40	12	23	27	27	30	38	16	7	45	27	30	36	39
33	35	17	20	18	23	29	11	6	34	19	22	27	29
Mean		23.0	27.7	28.5	30.2	38.0	18.0	6.2	48.0	27.2	28.7	37.5	37.5
Black													
38	66	22	26	20	25	30	13	11	41	28	32	33	40
45	68	18	22	16	23	27	13	10	31	21	25	25	32
43	70	16	21	14	23	27	12	9	31	19	23	23	30
39	75	22	27	19	30	34	14	16	38	25	29	29	36
44	80	11	18	11	21	25	10	8	27	16	20	20	26
Mean		17.8	22.8	15.8	24.4	28.6	12.4	10.8	33.6	21.8	25.8	26.0	32.4
Grand Mean		20.1	25.0	21.4	27.0	32.8	14.9	8.8	40.0	24.2	27.1	31.1	34.9

High School, a virtually all-black polling place, increased between the first primary and the run-off from 56 percent of the registered voters to 67 percent. (Arrington got 99 percent of this vote.)

But white conservatives also reacted to Arrington's strong showing in the primary by increasing their turnout. In the predominantly white precincts, turnout increased overall 7.8 percentage points between the first round and the run-off—almost double the increase in black precincts. At Highland Avenue Fire Station, a 98 percent white polling place, turnout increased by 22 percent (and Arrington's portion grew from 5 percent to 26 percent). In three of the white precincts—34, 40, and 32—turnout was 48 percent, 38 percent, and 37 percent, respectively, whereas in none of the black precincts was turnout higher than 34 percent. Since no special effort had been made to register the white population in response to black political success, the turnout figures (as opposed to the registration figures) suggest something akin to backlash.

Four years later, although the majority-white areas of the city continued to have higher turnout than the majority-black areas, the differences were much smaller. Turnout in all five majority-black precincts was higher than it had been in 1979. Only two white precincts showed an increase in 1983, and then only by 1 percentage point each. The *Birmingham News* reported a "record-breaking" black turnout of about 77 percent of registered voters, "about 10 percent higher than [the] white [turnout]."[29]

*B*lacks have gained political power in Birmingham, [and] this . . . has been accomplished with a decline in racial polarization, rather than an increase.

Conclusion

Birmingham has come a long way since the days of Bull Connor's police dogs and fire hoses. Two features of the change appear particularly noteworthy. First and most obviously, blacks have gained political power in Birmingham. There is now a black mayor, a black majority on the city council, and black representation on the county commission; and the voting power of Birmingham's blacks has been influential in statewide races, especially the 1986 race for the U.S. Senate. Second and perhaps more interestingly, this change in the distribution of political power has been accomplished with a decline in racial polarization, rather than an increase. Mayor Arrington has sought and gained significant white support.

The increased voting power of Birmingham's blacks apparently has been a function of numerous factors operating over a considerable period of time. The 1965 Voting Rights Act was certainly a trigger, and the relatively permissive attitude of the Jefferson County Board of Registrars also played a role. The kinds of strategies and efforts used to increase black voter registration were important as well. A variety of black organizations contributed to the gradual accumulation of political experience and the strengthening of the habit of participation. As we have seen, many of those organizations had broad purposes and did not focus their activities exclusively on electoral politics. In addition, many of their efforts were not closely coordinated amongst themselves. But collectively they gave rise to a broad-based organizational infrastructure upon which subsequent political gains could be built.

Political strategists may debate the relative merits of such loosely organized and broad-based efforts in comparison with efforts in which energies are single-mindedly directed at electoral success. The issue was probably moot in this case because the nature of many black organizations in Birmingham was already set when the 1965 Voting Rights Act put electoral power within reach. Moreover, the type of organization-building that had taken place in Birmingham seems in fact to have contributed to, and helped shape, subsequent political success. The non-electoral goals and activities were not only worthy in their own right, but they also provided the glue that held many of the organizations together between elections and during the period when electoral victories were few.

The second noteworthy change, the decline in racial polarization, seems to have been a function of the same organizational development that helped

Black organizers could be less political in appealing for members and support because black organizations had incentives other than political ones.

> *Black political power is well established [in Birmingham]—and will probably continue to be dominant as long as blacks join with whites in a biracial coalition.*

produce greater black voting power. Black organizers could be less political in appealing for members and support because black organizations had incentives other than political ones. That undoubtedly contributed to the lessening of racial polarization in Birmingham.

Richard Arrington helped bring about, and capitalized on, both of the significant changes. He helped found the Citizens Coalition in the mid-1970s to initiate a period of noticeable increases in black registration rates, and he appealed to enough whites to put together a majority coalition in his 1979 race for mayor, proving that a black could win and thereby sparking a dramatic rise in the black registration rate.

The long-range impact of the developments that have taken place in Birmingham since passage of the Voting Rights Act will be interesting to observe. Certainly, black political power is well established there—and will probably continue to be dominant as long as blacks join with whites in a biracial coalition. If an election were to be racially polarized, a black victory would be extremely problematic, because even though blacks now constitute 53 percent of Birmingham's registered voters, whites have a higher turnout rate.

Meanwhile, Mayor Arrington and others have founded a new organization that they hope will extend the approach taken by the Citizens Coalition to the rest of the state. Called the New South Coalition, the organization now boasts chapters in 40 of Alabama's 67 counties. It is explicitly biracial in membership, although whites are a decided minority. It is not irrevocably committed to the Democratic party, having split with the statewide Alabama Democratic Conference much as its parent organization did with the Jefferson County Progressive Democratic Council. And it intends to be more than a political organization. Among the issues addressed at a recent organizational meeting of one of its chapters was teenage pregnancy, for example.

The extent to which this broad-based, biracial approach will succeed in the variety of demographic and political settings found throughout the state is an open but very important question. Other organizational models have succeeded in other parts of the state, especially in localities where blacks constitute voting majorities, and it is natural for leaders to continue whatever approaches brought them to power in the first place. Differences in local organizational patterns will necessarily be reflected at the state level.

Certainly, Alabama politics is at a crossroads. Witness the 1986 election of the state's first Republican governor since Reconstruction at the same time that voters rejected an incumbent Republican U.S. Senator. The emergence of a meaningful two-party system is possible and credible. Both the nature of whatever system develops and the future political power of blacks within it depend heavily upon the organization and strategies of black political groups.

List of Persons Interviewed

Mary Babston, member of 1982 campaign staff of Democratic gubernatorial candidate George McMillan, Birmingham

Anita Boles, district director, office of Congressman Ben Erdreich, Birmingham

Jerome Gray, field director, Alabama Democratic Conference, Montgomery (interviewed by telephone)

Ben Green, president, Citizens Coalition; assistant to Mayor Arrington (interviewed by telephone)

Nell Hunter, chairman, Jefferson County Board of Registrars*

Simmie Lavender, former president, Citizens Coalition

Ornie McAlpin, deputy registrar, Jefferson County

Helen Moore, administrator of elections, state of Alabama

Don Siegelman, secretary of state, state of Alabama

Grover Smith, field director, Alabama NAACP, Birmingham

E. J. Stephens, former president, Birmingham League of Women Voters (interviewed by telephone)

Robert Thomas, field representative, staff of Congressman Ben Erdreich, Birmingham

Jarushia Thornton, state representative, 1982-83, Alabama District 44, Birmingham

Lewis White, office of the mayor, Birmingham (interviewed by telephone)

John Wilson, field representative, staff of Congressman Ben Erdreich, Birmingham

Abraham Woods, president, Birmingham SCLC

Even though the Jefferson County board consists of only one person, he or she bears the same title as that bestowed on selected members of the boards in all of Alabama's 62 other counties.

Endnotes

1. In 1986 the gubernatorial choice of Birmingham's black activists was again defeated, but black votes throughout the state contributed heavily to the election of Democrat Richard Shelby to the U.S. Senate.

2. Donald Strong, "Alabama—Transition and Alienation," in *The Changing Politics of the South,* ed. William C. Havard (Baton Rouge: LSU Press, 1972), p. 443.

3. Richard L. Engstrom and Michael McDonald, "The Election of Blacks to City Councils: Clarifying the Impact of Electoral Arrangements on the Seats/Population Relationship," *American Political Science Review,* 75 (June 1981), 344-354; Margaret K. Latimer, "Black Political Representation in Southern Cities: Election Systems and Other Causal Variables," *Urban Affairs Quarterly,* 15 (Sept. 1979), 65-86.

4. *Birmingham News,* Oct. 4, 1985.

5. With a nine-person council, Birmingham's minority at least had a greater possibility of being represented than did blacks in Birmingham's sister city of Mobile, where the governing commission has only three members. Mobile's commission was all white until 1985, when the court ordered the election of a council by districts.

6. In 1986, court action based on the Voting Rights Act of 1982 brought an order for the election of the commissioners by district. In November 1986, two blacks were elected to what had become a five-person body.

7. In this respect, the year 1986 was memorable. The Alabama Democratic Conference (the black arm of the state Democratic party) had been leading Alabama's black organizations in seeking, through court action, an end to at-large elections; in 1986 several city governments agreed to change from at-large to district elections and so did 18 of the state's 63 counties, including Jefferson. In every one of those jurisdictions, black representatives were elected in

1986 for the first time. Moreover, two blacks were elected to the state school board after redistricting.

8. Lester Salamon and Stephen Van Evera, "Fear, Apathy, and Discrimination: A Test of Three Explanations of Political Participation," *American Political Science Review*, 67 (Dec. 1973), 1288-1306; Sam Kernell, "Comment: A Re-Evaluation of Black Voting in Mississippi," *American Political Science Review*, 67 (Dec. 1973), 1307-1318.

9. Sidney Verba and Norman H. Nie, *Participation in America* (New York: Harper and Row, 1972), p. 171.

10. Douglas St. Angelo and Paul Puryear, "Fear, Apathy, and Other Dimensions of Black Voting," in *The New Black Politics*, eds. Michael Preston, Lenneal J. Henderson, and Paul Puryear (New York: Longman, 1982), p. 128.

11. Twiley W. Barker, "Political Mobilization of Black Chicago," *PS* (Summer 1983), p. 482.

12. Arrington's entrance into Birmingham politics provided the city's black citizenry with a leader whose qualifications for public office far exceeded those of most politicians of any race. He holds a doctorate in zoology from the University of Oklahoma (1966); taught at Miles College in Birmingham, where he became dean in 1967; was executive director of the Alabama Center for Higher Education from 1970-1979; and was first elected to the Birmingham City Council in 1971. In administrative experience and intellectual accomplishment, this native of Alabama was obviously no "ordinary politician."

13. *Birmingham News*, Oct. 10, 1979.

14. *Birmingham News*, Aug. 14, 1983.

15. *Birmingham News*, Oct. 12, 1983.

16. 320 F. Supp. 107 following *Dunn v. Blumstein* 405 U.S. 330.

17. In 1983 the national head of the Southern Christian Leadership Conference, Joseph Lowery, visited Governor Wallace to request more deputy registrars in Alabama. The visit resulted in the governor's sending a letter to the boards of registrars instructing them to increase the number of deputy registrars. Although the governor has no formal authority over county boards of registrars, his messages are still regarded as important.

18. In 1954 the NAACP was banned from Alabama as a "foreign corporation" and fined $100,000 a day for not revealing its membership lists. The U.S. Supreme Court overturned that decision in 1958. The temporary demise of the NAACP gave rise to other organizations of similar purpose.

19. The Alabama Democratic Conference was "attached" to the regular Democratic party during the chairmanship of Robert Vance, generally in defiance of the wishes of Governor Wallace.

20. Quoted in "God's Trombones," a series on Birmingham's black clergy by Sam Hodges, *Birmingham Post Herald,* Oct. 24, 25, 26, 1983.

21. The successful coalition of voters who elected Erdreich included not only blacks and labor, but also various people who had supported former liberal Republican Congressman John Buchanon but had never become enthusiastic about Smith. Buchanon represented the 6th district from 1964 until 1980, when Smith defeated him in the Republican primary. That year the Democrats, expecting Buchanon to be the Republican nominee, failed to put up a strong candidate.

22. *Birmingham News,* Oct. 16, 1983.

23. The data set includes registration figures for blacks and whites at the registration cutoff dates before the primary elections, the run-off primaries, and the general elections of 1978, 1980, and 1982. The data set also includes registration figures for blacks and whites at the cutoff dates for the primary elections for mayor and city council in 1979 and for the run-off primary in 1979. (Before the most recent court-approved reapportionment, Jefferson County's 21 precincts were also the state legislative districts.)

Voting totals include those for the primary elections, run-off primaries, and general elections for 1978, 1980, and 1982, and those for two city elections in 1979 and one in 1983. Figures for the state elections represent the number of voters in the race where turnout was highest (in 1978 and 1982, the gubernatorial race; in 1980, the presidential race).

24. The biggest problem with the Census data that were used involves totals of the black population in five predominantly white precincts (precincts 34, 35, 42, 49, and 50; all but the first are in outlying parts of the county). In those five precincts, we find black registration figures (even after re-identification) to be larger than the population reported by the Census Bureau. Since the number of black voters in the five precincts is small in relation to the total number of black voters in the county, we consider these precincts irrelevant to a study of black registration. We have therefore removed them from our general calculations whenever a division between blacks and whites contributes to a variable under study.

In addition, in precinct 37, a majority-black area, white population figures appear far too low and black figures are similarly questionable.

25. Our information on the voting-age population is based on general Census data.

In Jefferson County, a breakdown by age is not available by precinct. Thus, in order to derive the voting-age population for each precinct, we applied to all the precincts a formula derived from the voting-age population of the entire county (in 1980, 67.0 percent of the black population and 75.6 percent of the white population of Jefferson County was 18 years old and above).

Two other curiosities in the data should be mentioned. (1) Three of the 21 legislative precincts in Jefferson County (14, 15, and 52) include a few voters from neighboring counties. In analyzing Jefferson County, we subtracted these voters. (2) The city elections of 1979 and 1983 present the problem of unequal precinct populations because some precincts are wholly within the city and some are only partly within it. Because the city election is an at-large election, such variation in precincts has no effect on the city's final vote tally, but the variation does make it impossible to calculate accurate voting turnout for the entire city. For 1979 and 1983 we have omitted from consideration the 12 voting precincts that are wholly or partly outside the city limits; we have included the 9 that are wholly within the city. (Moreover, if we use a variable representing the percentage of black participation, we must also omit precinct 34 because of the faulty count of black population, see note 24.)

26. Since relatively few blacks registered before 1965, the number of whites purged because of long-time build-up on the registration lists was greater than the number of blacks.

27. As a result, the elected city commission in Bessemer, a majority-black community in precinct 41, was all white. Not until 1986, when Bessemer's at-large election law was challenged in court, did blacks have representation in that jurisdiction.

28. *Birmingham News,* Oct. 31, 1979.

29. *Birmingham News,* Oct. 12, 1983.

5. FROM POOL HALL TO PARISH HOUSE IN NORTH CAROLINA

Thomas F. Eamon

As the summer of 1982 settled over the tobacco fields of North Carolina's 2nd Congressional District, it appeared quite possible that a major shift would soon occur in the area's congressional representation. L. H. Fountain, described in *The Almanac of American Politics* as "the kind of politician who wears white linen suits in the summer time and speaks with a gentle southern courtliness the year round," had announced his retirement after 30 years in the U.S. House of Representatives.[1] On most economic and racial issues, Fountain had been typical of old-line conservative southern Democrats. In later years, even as many others were changing with the "new South," he continued to adhere to his principles.[2]

Shortly before the Democratic primary in June, the front runner appeared to be Henry McKinley (Mickey) Michaux (pronounced "mi-SHAW"), a black former state legislator from Durham. Some hoped and others feared that Michaux's election would herald sweeping change, real as well as symbolic. In fact, however, except for the all-important matter of race, he was quite a typical congressional candidate, albeit toward the left on the North Carolina political spectrum. His views placed him in the mainstream of post-World War II national Democrats, and his background in local politics was standard for a would-be congressman.

In the first Democratic primary, running against two whites, Michaux led by a substantial margin and won 44 percent of the vote. But in the run-off, he lost to his white opponent. Since Michaux's candidacy followed a pattern familiar to blacks who have run for office in North Carolina and elsewhere in the South, his story is an instructive chapter in the history of black attempts to win political office.

Michaux's candidacy followed a pattern familiar to blacks who have run for office in North Carolina and elsewhere in the South.

Background

Until a few months before the 1982 Democratic primary, no one knew what the make-up of North Carolina's 2nd Congressional District would be. The 1980 census had required some changes in the boundaries of the state's congressional districts in order to reflect modest shifts in population. In July 1981 the Democratic-controlled state legislature passed a redistricting bill, apparently with one goal in mind—to protect the incumbent members of the congressional delegation, whatever their party affiliation (seven were Democrats and four were Republicans). In earlier years, when the Democratic-controlled legislature adopted anti-Republican reapportionment plans, the tactic had backfired at the polls. This time, the reapportionment legislation seemed reasonably satisfactory to the state's congressional delegation. Ironically, however, the congressional map that was designed to make as few ripples as possible created waves of protest. The protest emanated from the NAACP, the state Republican party, and the U.S. Department of Justice.

Most of the dissatisfaction centered on the composition of the 2nd and 4th congressional districts, which were generally situated in the north central area of the state (see Figure 5-1). The 2nd district had long been associated with agricultural eastern North Carolina, a region that in many ways resembled the Deep South or the conservative Southside of Virginia. (Congressman Fountain came from Tarboro on the district's eastern edge.) Over the years, population shifts and the threat of federal court action had extended the 2nd district's boundaries deeply into an area of upland hills along the Virginia border known as the Piedmont. All the district's Piedmont counties except one—Orange County (Chapel Hill)—resembled its more conservative easterly areas in socioeconomic characteristics as well as in political outlook. (In Orange County, a coalition of academically-oriented liberals and blacks sometimes influenced elections.) Thus, Congressman Fountain's reputation as one of the South's most conservative Democrats appeared to stand him in good stead with a majority of voters in the 2nd district.

The federal government contended that racial considerations had induced the legislature to create the unusually shaped 2nd district for Fountain, presumably to avoid Durham's well-organized black vote.

Figure 5-1
North Carolina's 2nd and 4th Congressional Districts Before 1982

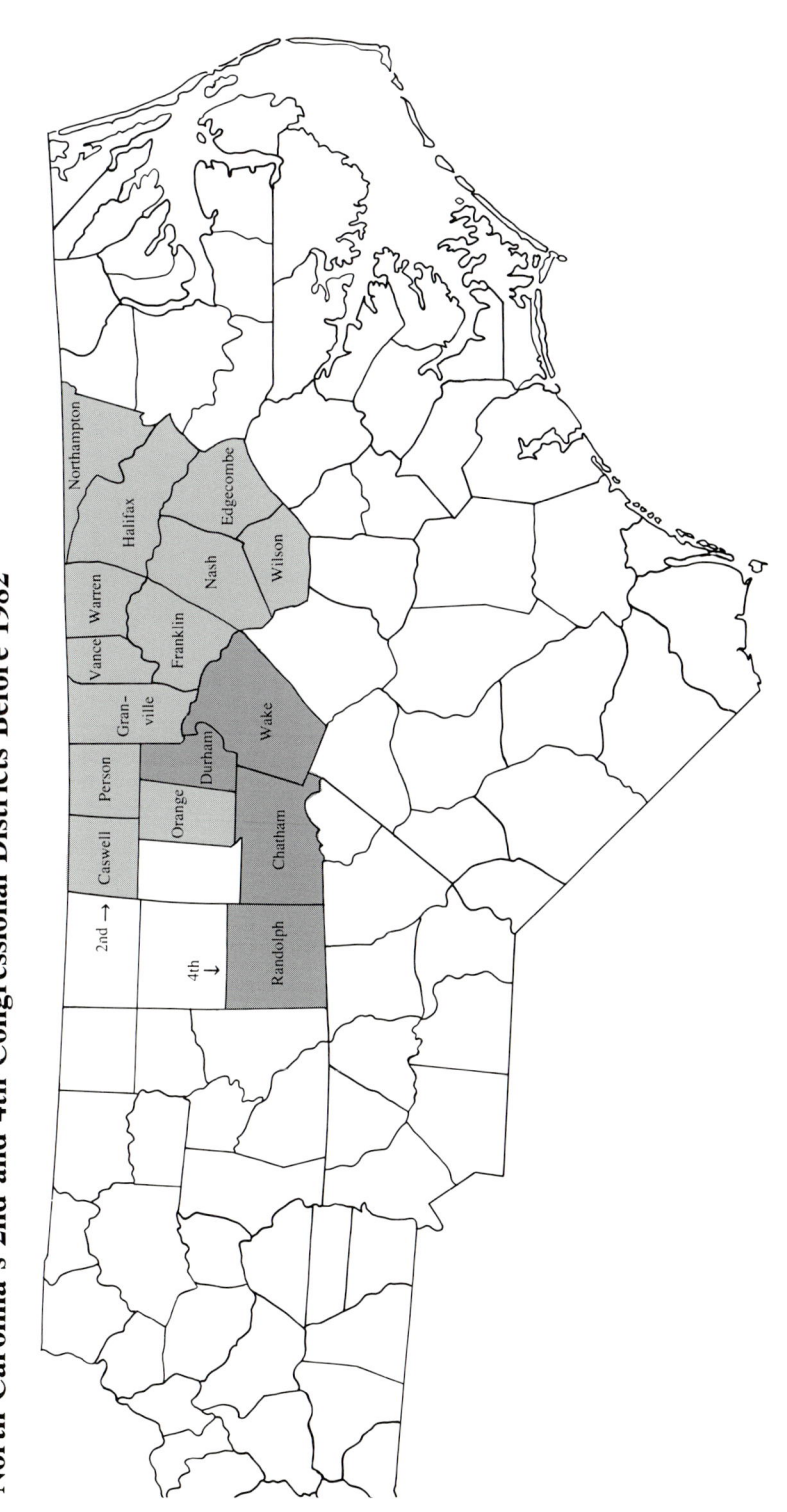

103

Michaux and his staff faced two major challenges: getting an unusually large black voter turnout, and overcoming the race barrier.

The 4th district, represented since 1972 by moderate Democrat Ike Andrews, had previously consisted of Durham, Wake, Chatham, and Randolph counties. Durham County consists of the city of Durham and its suburbs. Wake County includes the city of Raleigh; Chatham County is where Andrews lived until the early 1980s, when he moved to Wake; and Randolph is a Republican county that was at the western end of the district.

The 1981 reapportionment plan attempted to protect Fountain by drawing the 2nd district's boundary lines in such a way as to avoid the urban centers of Durham and Raleigh, with their reputed concentrations of liberals and Republicans. This required considerable ingenuity and resulted in a district temporarily labeled "Fountain's Fishhook" (see Figure 5-2).[3] Had that reapportionment plan gone into effect, a traveler from Durham would have been able to reach Fountain's 2nd district by driving north, south, east, or west.

The NAACP and the North Carolina Republican party filed lawsuits challenging the legislature's plans for congressional reapportionment and for state House and Senate districts. On December 8, 1981, before the courts ruled on the complaints, the Civil Rights Division of the U.S. Department of Justice struck down the congressional plan. Acting under provisions of the Voting Rights Act of 1965, the federal government contended that racial considerations had induced the legislature to create the unusually shaped 2nd district for Fountain, presumably to avoid Durham's well-organized black vote.[4]

Rather than contest the ruling, the legislature held a special session in February 1982 and adopted another plan, which the Justice Department approved on March 10 (see Figure 5-3).[5] The realigned 2nd district joined Durham County to nine counties already in Fountain's territory.[6] The incorporation of Durham introduced a new element into the 2nd district's otherwise largely rural and small-town constituency. Previously the two largest towns in the district were Rocky Mount and Wilson, with populations of 41,000 and 34,000, respectively. Durham (the city) has a population of 100,538. Moreover,

BACKGROUND

Figure 5-2
Plan Adopted by State Legislature in 1981 and Rejected by U.S. Department of Justice (2nd and 4th Congressional Districts, North Carolina)

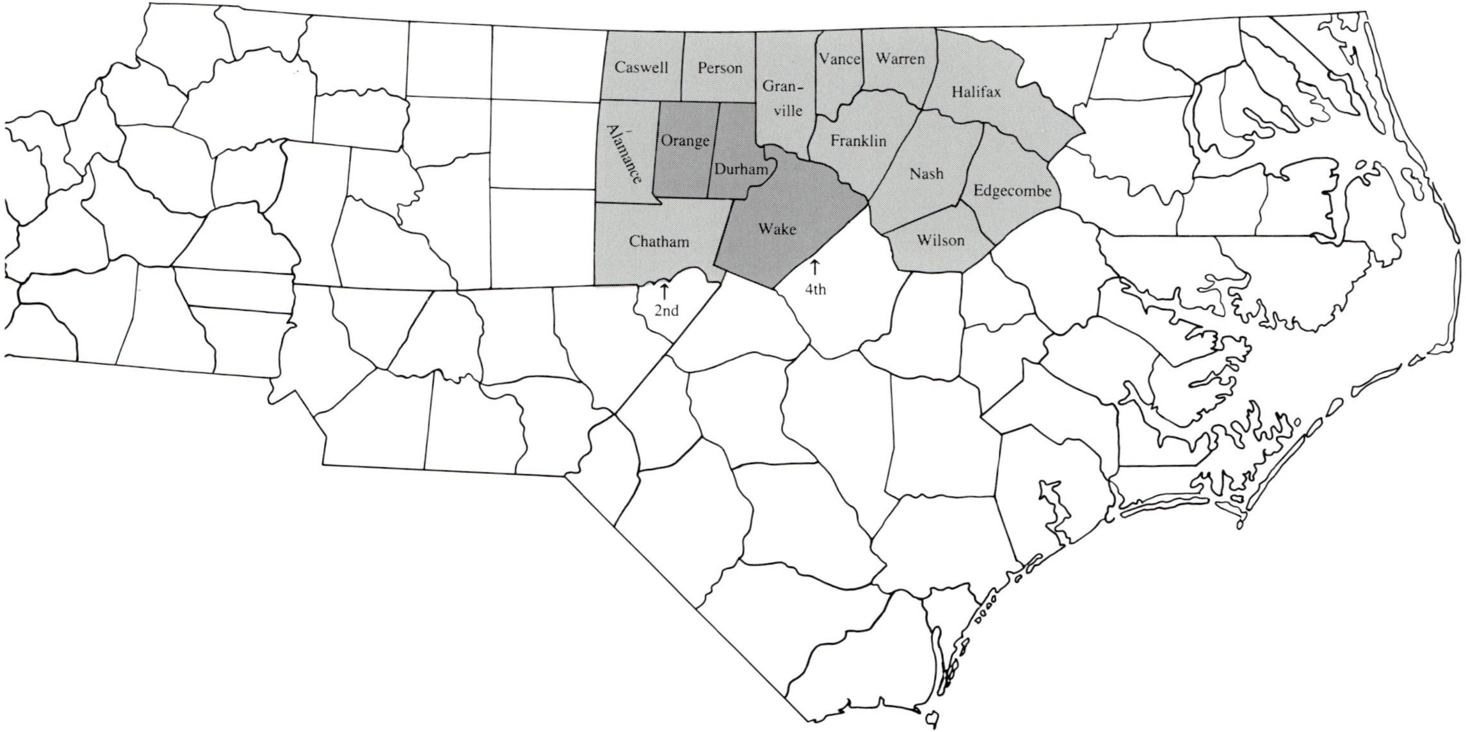

105

Figure 5-3
North Carolina's 2nd and 4th Congressional Districts, 1982–Present

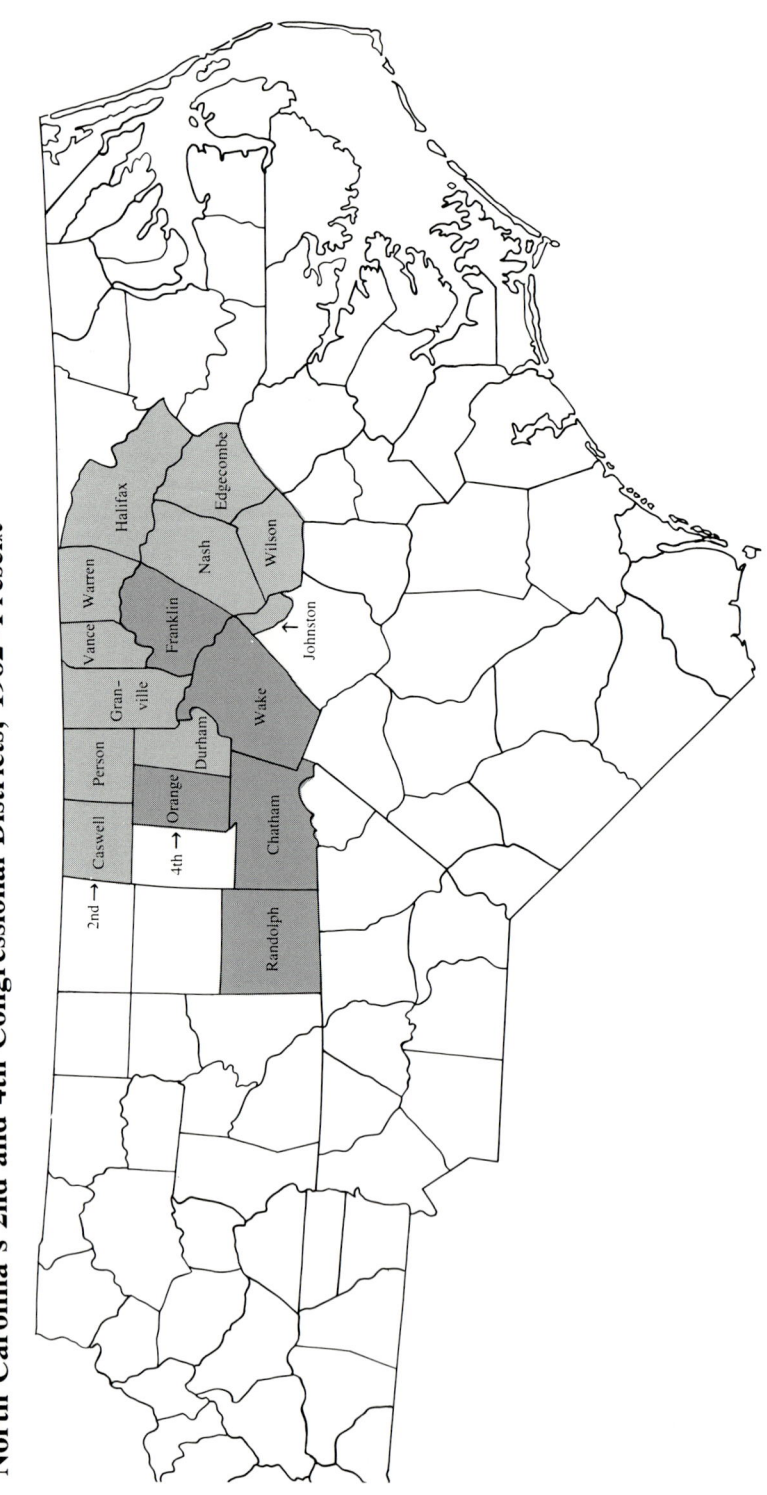

among North Carolina politicians Durham has a reputation for being liberal, and its well-organized black vote has become almost legendary. In actual size, however, that vote, which was about 30 percent of the total number of registered voters in the county in 1982, was smaller than many people supposed. (Two years later the black proportion of registered voters would rise dramatically. See note 11.)

With close to 30 percent of the district's voters now from Durham County, on March 27 the 69-year-old Fountain announced his retirement.

Five days before Fountain's announcement, Mickey Michaux became the first candidate to announce for the seat. For months, he had been ready to run in either the 2nd or the 4th district and to challenge either Fountain or Andrews, depending on where Durham ended up as a result of reapportionment; he preferred Durham to be in the 2nd district because of that district's concentration of rural blacks.

A 51-year-old attorney and the member of an affluent family that owned a number of business enterprises, Michaux had been elected three times (1972, 1974, 1976) as one of Durham's three at-large members in the state House of Representatives, after making three unsuccessful attempts to win the same office. Once elected, he was regarded as a good vote-getter and an important political force, and he played a major role in swinging much of Durham's black vote to moderately conservative U.S. Senate candidate Robert Morgan in the latter's 1974 victory. An early Carter supporter, Michaux served as a U.S. district attorney in the late 1970s.

Although calling himself a "fiscal conservative," Michaux made it clear from the beginning that the Reagan administration would be a target in the campaign. His policy differences with the administration on a wide range of issues, coupled with his color, made many district voters consider him a liberal.

After Fountain's withdrawal, there was much speculation about other candidates. On April 15, Itimous Thaddeus (Tim) Valentine, 56, from Nash in the eastern part of the district, became the second to

A massive voter registration drive became the sine qua non of Michaux's campaign.

The Michaux staff worked closely with organizations in the black community, especially churches and housing tenant organizations.

announce. An attorney, Valentine was the son of a state Supreme Court justice. He served three terms in the state legislature during the 1950s and was chairman of the state Democratic party from 1966 to 1968. In general, his political associations were with the business-oriented conservatives of the North Carolina Democratic party. The press would portray Valentine as the most conservative candidate in the race. Yet he supported renewal of the Voting Rights Act and argued that federal environmental laws should not be weakened. Valentine was considered a favorite son by many white voters in the eastern portion of the district and was supported by the Fountain organization.[7]

A third candidate, who announced his candidacy two weeks after Valentine, was former state House speaker James Edward Ramsey, 50, from rural Person County in the northwestern part of the district. Although regarded as something of a young Turk when he entered politics in the late 1950s, Ramsey had compiled a generally conservative record in the state House. He emphasized the need for industrial development in the district, gave a cautious endorsement to the proposed extension of the Voting Rights Act, and was portrayed as the centrist or moderate candidate in the race. Unlike Michaux and Valentine, he had little built-in geographic or organizational support. His strongholds tended to be in the most sparsely populated counties of the district. But he hoped to run well among whites in urban Durham, which borders his home county.

On April 28, the same day Ramsey announced, the state legislature met in a second special session and adopted a plan for state House and Senate seats that met with Justice Department approval. The plan set June 10 as the date for the first primary, with the run-off coming four weeks later. On April 30, however, the Justice Department rejected the June 10 date on the grounds that black legislative candidates (whose rights were being protected under the Voting Rights Act) would not have enough time to wage campaigns. On May 2, the state board of elections declared that primaries would be held Tuesday, June 29; any necessary run-offs would be held Tuesday, July 27. The Justice Department did not object. Eight weeks of campaign time remained in a district whose boundaries had been known for less than two months.

The Michaux Strategy

In its simplest form, the Michaux campaign strategy called for winning massive support from blacks in all parts of the district and combining that with support from whatever white voters, especially in urban Durham, might find his candidacy appealing. Such an approach, which is common enough in modern southern elections, tends not to work if blacks constitute less than a majority of the adult population. Michaux and his advisers could look to few examples of success in constituencies whose populations are racially similar to the population of North Carolina's 2nd district. (Blacks constitute 40 percent of the district's total population and 36 percent of its adult residents.) Thus, Michaux and his staff faced two major challenges: getting an unusually large black voter turnout, and overcoming the race barrier.

In aiming for a large black turnout, Michaux's staff assumed that an overwhelming percentage of all black votes would go to Michaux. As a candidate seeking black votes, he had many advantages. Well-known to black political elites, he would have an entree to all parts of the district. No other black was seeking the seat. He was a good speaker and sometimes a dynamic campaigner, and was respected as a former state legislator and federal district attorney. Whatever the odds offered by a detached observer, blacks (as well as whites) saw him as a serious candidate. (Moreover, wealthy by most standards, he could lend his campaign a substantial sum.) Thus, his first challenge was not so much getting the black vote as it was registering new black voters and then making certain that they exercised the franchise.

The black level of registration (41 percent of the black voting-age population and 27 percent of all registered voters in the district) was impressive when compared with the levels at earlier elections, but it was far from high enough to elect a congress-

In a sense, local registration officials also played a role in the registration drive, since election laws in North Carolina give county election boards some discretion in carrying out state law.

man. If whites voted at their usual off-year rate and blacks voted more heavily than usual, the black vote would provide a good base for Michaux.[8] But whites might vote at a higher level than usual. Pragmatic campaign considerations therefore dictated beginning a voter education and registration campaign almost immediately. A massive voter registration drive became the sine qua non of Michaux's campaign.

The race barrier represented perhaps an even greater challenge. Whites in the rural and small-town counties of the 2nd district were considered among the most race-conscious voters in North Carolina. Because the 2nd district is one of the few areas of the state where, over time, blacks have been a majority or a very large minority (40 percent or more) of the population, whites often have attitudes reminiscent of those held by whites in the Deep South "Black Belt." Outside Durham County, Michaux could count upon little open white support and probably less than 10 percent of the total white vote.

The situation in Durham County (over two-thirds of whose registered voters were white) was different. Many of Durham's white voters had cast votes for Michaux (along with two whites) in at-large races for the county's three seats in the state House. From his political as well as business and professional activities, Michaux had many connections in the white community. To some degree, Duke University and related facilities (mainly research facilities and institutes) had increased the liberal as well as the nonsouthern ranks in the city's white community. Labor unions were stronger than in much of the South. Yet, in the past whites in Durham had been more likely to vote along racial lines than had whites in other large North Carolina cities.

The Michaux campaign staff . . . targeted their drive at blacks with lower levels of income and education.

Voter Registration

Organizational Dynamics

Once the district lines were established, the local offices of Michaux's formal campaign organization quickly fell into place. Insofar as time permitted, campaign coordinators worked aggressively on registration, concentrating on local appearances by the candidate. In addition, much of the coordinators' efforts involved advising and encouraging local and nonpartisan groups that were working on registration.[9] The Michaux staff worked closely with organizations in the black community, especially churches and housing tenant organizations; they also worked closely with local black candidates in Edgecombe and Warren counties, which were two of the three counties where black candidates for local office were making especially strong efforts. (The third was Caswell, where the registration effort was largely left to the local black political organizations.)

Among groups not directly tied to the Michaux campaign, the A. Philip Randolph Institute played the biggest role in voter registration. The Randolph Institute is a national nonpartisan organization that does not endorse candidates. However, it was founded in 1964 to encourage cooperation between the black community and the labor movement; it professes an interest in building coalitions for social reform; and it attempts to work with established local groups that share its interests. Since its inception, the institute has emphasized voter registration as a means of promoting civil rights. To the Randolph Institute, North Carolina presented a golden opportunity.

[Michaux] went to pool rooms and barbecue pits . . . [and] many churches.

The employees of the institute ran their efforts independently of the Michaux campaign, stressing registration rather than electioneering. According to James Andrews, who went on leave from his job as a field worker with the North Carolina AFL-CIO to work with the Randolph Institute in its voter registration drive, the institute paid salaries to 8-10 persons to work in the 2nd district; gave small expense allowances to a few others; and used an estimated 50 volunteers.

Other groups not directly tied to the Michaux campaign also helped with registration. In some counties, black organizations such as the NAACP were a factor. Most of the counties also have black

A major task of the Randolph Institute was convincing potential voters that registration would present them with an opportunity while putting them under no obligation.

political action committees that endorse and sometimes actively support candidates for office, and some of those organizations (such as the Citizens for a Better Edgecombe County) were active in the registration drive. In addition, in rural and heavily black Caswell and Warren counties, local political action groups emphasized registration.

The powerful Durham Committee on the Affairs of Black People put only a limited effort into signing up voters for the June primary (Michaux believed they could have been more active), although its membership was involved in other phases of Michaux's campaign and the campaigns of blacks who were running within Durham County. Neighborhood groups in Durham did register voters.

In a sense, local registration officials also played a role in the registration drive, since election laws in North Carolina give county election boards some discretion in carrying out state law. For example, even though current state law permits a practice often favored by groups that mount major registration drives (the practice of using roving registrars, who may take applications at street corners, shopping centers, or other points), it allows individual county election boards to decide whether and how the practice is to be put into effect. Some local boards have accepted and used the practice, whereas others have been wary of it. A local board's position often reflects the views of the local office holders, party officials, and other influential individuals—but this may result in an attitude more favorable to blacks than an outsider would suspect. White officials sometimes see an increase in the black vote as being helpful to their own political races. In one of the counties of the 2nd district, Governor James B. Hunt's organization is thought to have encouraged black registration as a means of strengthening his own 1984 bid for a seat in the U.S. Senate.[10] (County election boards may also be influenced by the availability of funds and personnel.)

Outreach Activities

The Michaux campaign staff believed that most middle-class blacks had already registered. Therefore, they targeted their drive at blacks with lower levels of income and education. When interviewed after the campaign, Michaux said,

> We were primarily interested in "grassroots" voters, though I hate to use the term—those moderate- to low-income people who would not normally participate. We knew the people in housing projects were less registered than others. We would go into neighborhoods and knock on doors. I visited every housing project in the district. We used a Winnebago recreation vehicle. Our reception was very good. . . . Also, I went to pool rooms and barbecue pits. I'd shoot a little pool.

In housing tenant organizations, where there was a relatively large pool of unregistered persons, announcements relating to registration were made in meetings of the tenant organizations. A door-to-door approach was also used. The efforts were most fruitful when the candidate himself visited a particular project, often accompanied by leaders of the tenant organization.

In the pool rooms, the candidate usually started out chatting with the customers. After a few minutes, the conversation might move to topics of registration and voting. There and in the housing projects, Michaux generally met a good response to his appeal, but when walking the lines outside unemployment offices, where he often encountered whites as well as blacks, he found more bitterness and cynicism.

Michaux also went to many churches, reporting later that he "worked three churches a Sunday." Some of the churches that played a role in the registration drive tied their appeals directly to the Michaux campaign; others were more discreet. When the candidate visited, on some occasions he was invited to address the congregation. At other times, the minister simply announced his presence and his availability to talk with parishioners, and then after the service Michaux greeted prospective registrants and others in the lobby, basement, or annex. On a few occasions, receptions were held in his honor. Michaux said afterward that most active church

County election boards were both cooperative and recalcitrant.

members were probably already registered to vote but that a church visit was worthwhile if it increased registration by 10 or 15 persons. In addition, the candidate's presence undoubtedly gave the overall campaign a boost.

By a fluke, the Michaux campaign had another technique for targeting unregistered voters. One of the key strategists for the campaign was James O'Reilly, a former state employee who had been able to obtain a master list of licensed drivers. Although forbidden to sell the list, he was able to use it in his own work as a political consultant to Michaux. With a computer, he matched the lists of licensed drivers with lists of registered voters, identifying the licensed drivers who were unregistered.

In the early stages of the campaign, the Michaux staff used radio messages on black-oriented stations. (Radio was the only mass medium that was used to encourage registration.) One spot—the only radio ad directed specifically at registration—had the theme, "A Right You Don't Use Is a Right You Can Lose." The spot suggested that voters would have a "real choice" in the upcoming election but that a person had to register in order to vote. Later spots went to general as well as black-oriented stations. One was lifted from Michaux's statement announcing his candidacy and, although designed to appeal to a more general audience, was also expected to create interest among blacks and indirectly increase black registration. It emphasized the needs of the district. Another spot drew a connection between Michaux's recent experience as a district attorney and his ability to fight crime.

*B*etween *[February] and June, about 17,000 blacks registered, for an increase of 29 percent. This was quite spectacular in a largely rural and small-town section of North Carolina.*

Like the Michaux organization, the A. Philip Randolph Institute made use of personal and group contact, especially the latter. Among the groups appealed to were church congregations, tenant steering committees, and social groups such as motor van clubs.

The institute's registration efforts also featured printed leaflets. Some people discounted their value, but James Andrews argued that "it's a good conversation piece if done the right way." He noted that among the members of a typical street corner group, several might view any political message with cynicism but at least one or two might say, "It has a point." Those few might then register and even encourage others to do likewise.

The Randolph Institute flyer pictured slain civil rights workers and leaders like Martin Luther King, Jr., with a message that began, "They died for you." Because the institute is nonpartisan, the flyer was not created specifically for the Michaux campaign. It was, though, prepared for distribution in the North Carolina 2nd, and as an all-purpose document it was used there in a variety of situations.

In the conversations Andrews held with potential black voters in the district, he used three major messages to overcome apathy toward registering. First, he reminded those he was speaking with that blacks had not always had the opportunity to participate in politics and so they should take full advantage of it now. Second, he advised them that regardless of the stories they might have heard about registration in the past, registering is relatively simple today. A third hurdle, he said, involved uncertainty, especially among uneducated or younger people, about what to expect once they registered. Thus, a major task of the Randolph Institute was convincing potential voters that registration would present them with an opportunity while putting them under no obligation.

County election boards were both cooperative and recalcitrant. The Michaux campaign coordinator in Wilson County reported that the election board was quite cooperative in providing for roving registrars on street corners, where Michaux workers and sometimes the candidate himself would be on hand, urging the unregistered to sign up. In nearby Edgecombe County, local officials contended that they lacked the funds to pay registrars for extra duties. Eventually, however, a system was set up by which an interested organization could pay the county 50 cents for each new voter registered in a special drive. Under state law the payment could not be made by a candidate or a partisan organization, but it could be provided by a group such as the Citizens

The largest minority increases occurred in the rural and small-town counties where blacks constitute from 40 to 60 percent of the total population.

Grassroots activity for local candidates helped boost registration to the advantage of Michaux's district candidacy.

for a Better Edgecombe. Michaux was under the impression that the payment made for this service in Edgecombe came indirectly from his campaign.

Also in Edgecombe County, the location of a registration table was a source of contention on at least one occasion. The election board turned down a request to register voters at church on Sundays. The practice of registering voters at church on Sundays, however, was common in other counties in the district.

Effectiveness

For the 10 counties entirely within the 2nd district, the pre-election registration breakdown by race between May 1981 and June 1982 is shown in Table 5-1. Serious registration efforts for Michaux's

Table 5-1

Pre-Election Registration, 2nd District (North Carolina), by Race

	May 1981	Feb. 1982	March 1982	June Primary 1982	% Increase Feb. to June 1982
Blacks	56,663	57,765	61,995	74,511	29.0
Whites	146,830	146,980	148,168	153,744	4.6

planned campaign and for local races involving black candidates began in February 1982. Between then and June, about 17,000 blacks registered, for an increase of 29 percent. This was quite spectacular in a largely rural and small-town section of North Carolina with a tradition of low minority participation. In these terms, the registration drive in the 2nd district must be judged a success. Had a formal campaign organization been in place two months earlier, voter registration might have increased still more dramatically.

A county-by-county analysis (not shown) indicates that the largest minority increases occurred in the rural and small-town counties where blacks constitute from 40 to 60 percent of the total population. But black registration drives were also quite productive in the two semi-urban Valentine strongholds in the eastern part of the district, Nash and Wilson counties. The increase in Durham was a relatively modest 18 percent.[11]

Major gains in white registration took place in Caswell and Warren counties, where spirited local contests were being fought. But in the other counties, including some with heated interracial battles, whites registered in modest numbers.

In most counties, including Durham, the number of blacks who were registered was smaller than the number of whites, but the gap was significantly narrower than in the past. In Caswell and Warren counties, both of which had a history of conservative white rule, eligible blacks were now just as likely to be registered as were eligible whites—an unusual phenomenon in the United States.[12]

The groups involved in voter registration activities did not evaluate their own efforts, but other data and interviews allow us to reach some conclusions about the effectiveness of the various efforts.

Person-to-person contact, especially involving the candidate, was almost certainly a crucial factor in the registration drive. Michaux was a dynamic candidate and his candidacy clearly was a major catalyst. It might seem paradoxical in view of Michaux's wealth (he is a millionaire), but he seemed able to identify with moderate- and low-income blacks. And he made an effort to reach them.

The radio ads may or may not have been effective. Perhaps they stirred some interest, but the extent of it is undocumented and their net effect is difficult to judge. Michaux and his campaign workers thought the ad relating to registration was important. The ad on fighting crime probably had little effect on voter registration.

The policy of the state government [encouraged black registration and] made a significant difference.

Civic groups and churches probably had a more substantial impact on voter education than on actual registration, probably because the members of such groups were more likely than not to be already registered. Still, those organizations did serve as part of a network spreading word of the Michaux effort.

Grassroots activity for local candidates helped boost registration to the advantage of Michaux's district candidacy. Blacks were serious contenders in heated county-level races from urban Durham to rural Warren. In three rural counties with strong black candidates seeking political office (Caswell, Edgecombe, and Warren), increases in voter registration were especially marked.

The impact of labor was more significant in later stages of the campaign. In-state and out-of-state labor groups were deeply involved, but much of their effort came too late to boost black registration. Exceptions were the A. Philip Randolph Institute and the North Carolina AFL-CIO, both of which provided research information that was valuable in targeting potential voters. In addition, the Randolph Institute had extensive contacts. Michaux credited it with playing a significant role in the registration drive.

Finally, the policy of the state government made a significant difference. In North Carolina, the governor exerts control over the state board of elections, which in turn influences policy at the county level. The administration of Governor Hunt maintained a policy of encouraging black registration, probably because Hunt intended to run in 1984 against conservative Republican Senator Jesse Helms. Thus, registering to vote is now easier than ever before in North Carolina. Registrars, once restricted to court houses and polling places, may now venture into public libraries or churches or even onto the streets.

As a whole, all these conclusions point in one direction: in the attempt to boost registration, there seems to be no substitute for person-to-person contact, whether made by the candidate's staff itself or by supporting organizations.

In the attempt to boost registration, there seems to be no substitute for person-to-person contact, whether made by the candidate's staff itself or by supporting organizations.

Voter Turnout

Organizational Dynamics

In the black get-out-the-vote (GOTV) effort, several groups other than the formal Michaux campaign organization were significant. They included—

- county-level black political action groups (for example, the Durham Committee on the Affairs of Black People);
- labor union support groups;
- PACE (Political Action Committee on Education), the political arm of the North Carolina Association of Educators; and
- the League of Conservation Voters.

County-Level Black Political Action Groups.
Perhaps of greatest significance were the county-level black political action groups, which have an influential organization in most counties in the district. Also in most counties—Wilson has been an exception in recent years—those organizations endorse candidates and attempt to turn out a good vote on election day. Their enthusiasm and effectiveness seem to be greatest when blacks are serious contenders for office.

As the primary approached, virtually all the existing organizations cooperated closely with the Michaux campaign. In Durham, Edgecombe, Caswell, and Warren, black GOTV efforts were especially successful. The Durham Committee on the Affairs of Black People, which had done little to encourage voter registration, mounted a major GOTV drive for Michaux as well as for incumbent black members of the county commission. The Citizens for a Better Edgecombe County augmented its registration efforts with an election-day drive for Michaux and local candidates. In Caswell County, at the request of local black political leaders, the existing structure rather than a major Michaux organization was put in charge of the voter drive; measured by past county voting standards, they produced good results. In Warren County, black political action groups appeared to be only as strong as the personalities of various leaders, but they, too, produced good results.

Perhaps of greatest significance [in the GOTV effort] were the county-level black political action groups.

The major GOTV effort was a phone bank operation in which various organizations participated....

Election-day activities consisted largely of getting loyal voters to the polls. "Haulers" or drivers were provided, and they used taxis, trucks, or private automobiles. Barbecues or similar events were held to feed campaign workers (and sometimes other politicians). These techniques are quite standard, but the various county black political action groups appear to have used them with special intensity for the Michaux campaign.

To support their election-day activities, the county-level organizations usually ask for contributions from endorsed candidates. In the primary and the run-off, the Michaux campaign contributed from $500 to $1,200 to each of the various political action groups, spending a grand total of $10,225 specifically on GOTV efforts.

Organized Labor. Although organized labor provided primarily financial and research assistance, some units helped in the GOTV effort. County-level coordinators indicated that national and local labor representatives worked largely among their own members. It would be difficult to assess their impact. However, Michaux gave particular credit to the "Operation Big Vote" drive of the American Federation of State, County, and Municipal Employees (AFSCME), who worked not only among their own members but also among other potential Michaux voters (see pages 123–124). Operation Big Vote operatives often came from outside the state and spread out into the neighborhoods.

Political Action Committee on Education (PACE). The members of PACE not only provided money but also were helpful in staffing phone banks, mostly in the Michaux campaign offices (see page 124). In some counties, the educators were just about the only visible white support for the campaign. Although national education groups backed Michaux, local units provided the manpower for the campaign.[13]

The League of Conservation Voters and Other Majority-White Groups. Still other groups worked mainly in the white community. Michaux applauded the League of Conservation Voters, whose "flying squads" worked among whites on a block-by-block basis. Other liberal white groups, such as the Durham Voters' Alliance and the People's Alliance, also worked primarily among their own members, and they provided their membership mailing lists to the Michaux campaign organization.

Outreach Activities

The major GOTV effort was a phone bank operation in which various organizations participated, with the actual operation and supervision normally taking place at Michaux headquarters. An extensive voter research and targeting program assured the efficiency of the phone drive. From county election boards Michaux headquarters had obtained computerized lists of each voter's address, race, party registration, and approximate age, and these proved useful in the phone drive.

As election day approached, campaign workers, union support groups, and education lobbies staffed the phone banks. Except in Durham, the effort was largely limited to blacks. Using the standard technique, the people manning the phone banks reminded voters of the election and urged them to support Michaux. Voters who needed rides were offered transportation. On election day itself, the phone banks played a key role. Kevin Smith, manager of Michaux's campaign, later regretted not having used them even more. (Lack of money was somewhat of a problem.)

Radio broadcasts also played a key role in the GOTV drive. Michaux was thought to have a commanding presence on the air, and radio rates were quite reasonable in the district, especially on small-town stations. The Michaux campaign spent $36,410 on radio—the category with the single highest expenditure in the total campaign budget of $300,000. Black radio was used extensively, but major metropolitan stations outside the district (including Raleigh's WPTF) were also used.

Media consultants urged that broadcasts be concentrated during workers' driving times. To some degree this advice was followed, but Kristen Peter-

Except in Durham, the effort was largely limited to blacks.

sen, Michaux's director of communications, argued that commuting patterns in the 2nd district were often different from those in urban centers. "Mill workers changing shifts and farmers often have different driving times and listening habits," she said. Consequently, the campaign devoted some resources to off-peak radio. Defending the use of radio, Petersen added that "it's very valuable, a one-to-one contact when a driver is in a car. It puts reminders in the head." No one in the campaign seemed to regret the use of radio. Some wished that the medium could have been used even more.

The money spent on television totaled $32,000. Initially, the campaign staff dismissed television as not being worth the expense in an oddly shaped district like the 2nd. Furthermore, television would expose Michaux's color to potentially hostile viewers and perhaps mobilize them to vote against him. Toward the end of the first primary campaign, however, strategists did resort to the use of television, and they continued using it through the campaign for the run-off.

*R**eflecting on the campaign later, three key Michaux strategists regretted not having spent more money on television in the campaign for the run-off.*

Two considerations played a role in the reversal. First, both the observations of campaign workers and the results of a professional poll indicated that many blacks were unaware of Michaux's candidacy. Campaign workers had seen a black in Person County with a Jim Ramsey sticker on his pick-up truck; on a more scientific level, the Cooper Associates poll in June indicated that more than half the district's blacks responded "not aware" or "not sure" when asked whether a black was running for Congress.[14] Since the campaign staff was assuming that Michaux would get almost unanimous support from blacks, poll analysts suggested the immediate use of television. Second, with both Ramsey and Valentine using television extensively in the closing days of the first-primary campaign, the Michaux forces felt competitive pressure to use the medium. Reflecting on the campaign later, three key Michaux strategists regretted not having spent more money on television in the campaign for the run-off. (The funds were not available, although if the staff had anticipated the need, perhaps they could have borrowed more money.)

Printed campaign materials were also used in the GOTV efforts. Various leaflets appealed to different categories of black and white voters, including the elderly. Letters about the campaign went to many voters. Some staff members considered the leaflets and letters to have been helpful, but no real documentation of their effect is available.

Finally, the extensive "black network," formal and informal, should not be overlooked. Most respondents emphasized its importance even when they had trouble pinpointing its exact nature. Perhaps that network can be traced back to the days when blacks had little access to the established media and devised alternative means of communicating. In those days, much of the black community would become informed about political events by word of mouth. Today, churches as well as fraternal and political organizations play a role in the network, which continues to be important even as blacks have gained a bit more access to traditional outlets. The black network enables verbal messages to be transmitted in relative secrecy—sometimes an important consideration in politics.

The extensive "black network," formal and informal, should not be overlooked. Most respondents emphasized its importance even when they had trouble pinpointing its exact nature.

Fund-Raising

Overall contributions made to the Michaux campaign by July 29, 1982, were as follows:

Political Action Committees (PACs)	
Union PACs	$51,235.36
All other PACs	21,850.00
Total	$73,085.36
Individuals	
Durham County	$ 38,148.20
2nd district excluding Durham	14,620.36
North Carolina outside 2nd district	36,206.30
Out-of-state	21,280.00
Total	$110,254.86
Unidentified (estimated)	$10,000.00

Organized Groups and PACs. Union PACs contributed a total of $51,235 to the campaign. But Michaux indicated that some of the most valuable union aid (especially from AFSCME) came in the form of representatives sent in to help turn out the vote on election day: "There is no way this help could be measured in money terms. It doesn't show up on the campaign reports, but it was worth a lot."

Among non-union PACs, the various affiliates of the National Education Association spent large sums on the campaign. And once again, the formal campaign reports fail to reveal the true magnitude of the help given. Michaux and many of his campaign aides spoke appreciatively of the affiliates' volunteer efforts. Michaux also applauded the efforts of the National Committee for an Effective Congress, which played a key role in lining up organizational support that would later be translated into contributions. In addition, he spoke of the League of Conservation Voters, which supplemented a modest financial contribution with extensive volunteer support. The latter two organizations also helped generate individual contributions from outside the state.

In sum, it is probably accurate to conclude that support from organized groups and their PACs was a much bigger factor in the campaign than the Federal Election Commission reports would indicate. Christopher Scott of the AFL-CIO in Raleigh suggested that such aid came, in part, because the possibility of a black's winning in such an unlikely spot as North Carolina's 2nd district "captured the imaginations" of interest-group leaders. Michaux's effort was seen as heroic. On a more pragmatic level, interest-group leaders saw a fairly good chance to replace the conservative Fountain with someone sympathetic to their views.

Some of the most valuable union aid (especially from AFSCME) came in the form of representatives sent in to help turn out the vote on election day.

Individuals. In terms of fund-raising from individuals, perhaps the biggest disappointment to the Michaux forces was Durham. Prospects there had been considered excellent. Durham—the candidate's home town—has a black business and professional infrastructure that is probably unmatched in any other middle-sized city in the United States. It includes a number of black millionaires and many other blacks of substantial means. The leaders of Michaux's general county campaign were a highly regarded black bank executive and a prominent white attorney, both of whom spent some time raising money. The co-chairs of the general finance committee—although their roles were, in part, titular—included a prominent black Durham business leader with national connections and a white woman descended from the Duke tobacco family. But Eric Michaux, the candidate's brother and key adviser, said, "It was hard to get people in Durham excited. Whites were polite but didn't produce. Many blacks operated on a business-as-usual basis."

Several persons involved with finance said that most black U.S. business and professional people simply were not in the habit of contributing large sums of money: "They think a contribution of $20, $50, or $100 is huge. It's hard to get them to think in terms of $1,000." It was further suggested that such an attitude must change if blacks are to have an independent base from which to seek political office. On the surface, Durham would seem to be a good place for the change in attitude to start. But in Durham that change has been slow in coming.

The various affiliates of the National Education Association spent large sums on the campaign. And once again, the formal campaign reports fail to reveal the true magnitude of the help given.

Effectiveness

The results of the June 29 first-round primary are presented in Table 5-2. A county-by-county analysis (not shown) reveals that Michaux won a 5,600 vote majority in his native Durham and pluralities in five other counties. Valentine scored heavily in his eastern home base. Ramsey ran well in his home territory, near the Virginia border.

Table 5-2

Results of First-Round and Run-Off Primaries (2nd District, North Carolina)

	First Round		Run-Off	
Candidate	Vote Received	Percentage of the Total Vote Cast	Vote Received	Percentage of the Total Vote Cast
Michaux	47,132	44.5	51,056	46.5
Valentine	34,708	32.7	58,833	53.5
Ramsey	24,179	22.9		

In terms of fundraising from individuals, perhaps the biggest disappointment to the Michaux forces was Durham.

For the run-off, many political observers placed the odds at about 50-50. Both Valentine and Michaux thought much would hinge on a get-out-the-vote effort. After a sometimes heated four-week campaign (with most of Ramsey's key workers having switched to Valentine), Valentine emerged as the victor by a substantial margin (see Table 5-2).

A county-by-county analysis (not shown) reveals that Michaux's share of the vote in Durham rose slightly, from 58 percent in the first round to 59 percent in the run-off. In heavily black Warren County, Michaux was able to garner 55 percent of the vote; in Edgecombe, barely 50 percent.[15] Everywhere else Valentine won, with totals ranging from 52 percent in Caswell County to more than 68 percent in his native Nash.

A most remarkable feature of the run-off was the 3,900 increase in the total vote, from 106,010 to 109,914. Voter turnout increased in all counties except Michaux's Durham and Ramsey's Person, both of which experienced slight drop-offs. Michaux's total grew by approximately 3,900, and Valentine received only 54 votes less than the Valentine-Ramsey total in the first primary. Given the well-established racial voting patterns in the area, it seems reasonable to assume that most Ramsey supporters voted for Valentine and that, as this analysis will suggest, the modest increase in the Michaux total came from blacks rather than whites.

In North Carolina, participation is usually much lower in run-offs than in first-round primaries because of the drop in the number of races and, perhaps, an increase in voter apathy or boredom. Indeed, in many counties outside the 2nd district, the July 27 turnout was the lowest in North Carolina history (the only statewide run-off was in two Appeals Court elections). Even in Mecklenburg, which is the state's largest county and lies outside the 2nd district, the total vote was less than the total vote in sparsely populated counties that lie inside the 2nd district. The increase in the 2nd district was all the more remarkable considering that the second primary was held during the summer "dog days." Michaux said later, "We were surprised; we thought the white turnout would be much lower."

A natural question to ask is what role race might have played in sustaining and increasing voter interest. In this well-publicized election, the media had focused on Michaux's attempt to become the "first black" to represent North Carolina in Congress since the turn of the century. Both campaigns, Michaux's and Valentine's, made use of the racial issue in subtle ways when appealing to their potential supporters, although it should be emphasized that both candidates appeared uncomfortable with the situation.

Analysis of turnout in terms of aggregate data is difficult, since most voting districts outside Durham County are mixed in their racial composition, as is true generally of the rural and small-town South. And making inferences about individual voting behavior on the basis of aggregate totals should be done cautiously. Nevertheless, the official voting returns provide some interesting clues to turnout and to possible shifts between the first primary and the run-off.

Looking first at Durham, which the Michaux forces called a "disappointment," we find that the Michaux total dropped about 2.4 percent from 15,917 to 15,540 and that Valentine, even while apparently gaining most of Ramsey's votes, still had a total (10,750) that was about 5 percent lower than the combined Valentine-Ramsey vote (11,318) in the first primary. These drops are very minor in comparison with the usual drop between primaries, which is substantial.

Here a more detailed scrutiny is possible because many precincts in Durham, unlike precincts in most of the other counties in the district, are fairly homogeneous in race. The registration figures for the primaries indicate that in 7 Durham precincts (where 45 percent of all the county's registered blacks live), blacks constituted 90 percent or more of the registered voters; most of those precincts were almost 100 percent black. In 13 Durham precincts (where 42 percent of the county's registered whites live), whites constituted 90 percent or more of the registered voters; most of those precincts fell around the 95 percent mark.

A most remarkable feature of the run-off was the 3,900 increase in the total vote, from 106,010 to 109,914.

A close look at voting patterns in those 20 relatively homogeneous precincts reveals a picture somewhat different from what one might have expected. There was high black turnout in both primaries. Indeed, in the heavily black precincts, voter participation as a percentage of registrants increased from 62.1 percent in June to 64.4 percent in the July run-off. This seems to conflict with the assumption made by some observers that in Durham, black voter interest decreased from the first to the second primary. In fact, in both elections the turnout in black precincts was abnormally high for an off year. In the first primary, a number of Durham blacks were seeking county-level office. But in the run-off, the major drawing card was the Michaux candidacy, and in these precincts Michaux's vote increased from 5,138 in the first round to 5,345 in the run-off. The vote for his white opponents was miniscule. The combined Valentine-Ramsey total was 89 votes in the first round, and Valentine received only 71 votes in the run-off.

The 13 white precincts present an equally interesting picture. For the first primary, voter participation was at the moderate and quite normal level of 47.6 percent of registration. Although turnout for the run-off was down slightly from to 44.5 percent, it would have been down much more in the absence of a heated congressional race. The vote for Valentine dropped to 4,959 from the combined Valentine-Ramsey total of 5,083 in the first primary. But Michaux's vote dropped more, from 2,247 in the first round to 1,920 in the run-off.

In both elections the turnout in black precincts [in Durham] was abnormally high for an off year.

Several conclusions seem warranted. (They apply mainly to the 20 homogeneous precincts rather than to the county as a whole, but using those 20 precincts is our only way of isolating black and white voters for analysis.) First, in the 20 precincts, black and white voter interest was reasonably high for a mid-summer primary, but clearly blacks were the more highly motivated. Second, white Ramsey voters switched in massive numbers to Valentine; almost none went to Michaux. Third, Durham whites—unlike whites elsewhere in the district—voted in significant numbers for Michaux. But the white Michaux vote appears to have slipped somewhat between primaries. This could have been simply a normal falling-off, with white Michaux backers feeling less of a stake in the election than black supporters felt. Or a few of Michaux's white supporters could have stayed home (or switched)— in response to Valentine's attack on what the area's whites call "bloc voting" among blacks, or as an expression of some objection to the Michaux campaign. It seems doubtful that many of the whites who voted for Michaux in the first place would be sensitive to a subtle racial campaign, but certainly a few could have been.

Outside Durham, this type of precinct analysis is less revealing, but the overall data by county provide some clues. In the four eastern counties of the district, where Valentine was regarded by many whites as a "home boy" and where white racial attitudes have been historically conservative, Valentine's run-off vote of 29,784 was 14.1 percent higher than the combined Valentine-Ramsey vote of 26,021 in the first primary (see Table 5-3). This was most probably due to increased white mobilization and was perhaps a reaction to black political activity (blacks made an intensive effort to get out the vote, perhaps sensing that Michaux had a good chance of winning). Michaux's vote increased in the same four counties by 10.3 percent, going from 17,914 to 19,861. Thus, among blacks as well as whites in the eastern counties, the run-off vote re-

Among blacks as well as whites in the eastern counties, the run-off vote reflects greater interest than there was in the first primary.

Table 5-3
Turnout in Eastern Counties (2nd District, North Carolina)

	First Primary			Second Primary		
County	Michaux	Valentine-Ramsey Total	Turnout as % of Regis.	Michaux	Valentine	Turnout as % of Regis.
Edgecombe	5,603	5,428	54.6	5,993	5,886	62.1
Halifax	5,094	6,188	51.8	5,145	6,895	55.3
Nash	3,283	7,791	50.8	4,070	8,882	59.5
Wilson	3,934	6,614	48.4	4,653	8,121	58.6
Total	17,914	26,021	51.9	19,861	29,784	58.8

flects greater interest than there was in the first primary.

The pattern in the five counties along the Virginia border—similar in racial orientation to the eastern counties but more rural—was slightly different (see Table 5-4). Here the second primary vote for Valentine (19,647) was down 7.7 percent from the Valentine-Ramsey total (21,291) in the first primary, probably reflecting decreased participation among Ramsey voters. But except in Ramsey's Person County, the total voter turnout was up—because the Michaux vote increased an astonishing 22.2 percent, going from 13,237 to 16,179. Although Michaux won a majority only in heavily black Warren County, in all five of the Virginia-border counties his raw vote totals rose sharply. In these counties as in Durham, therefore, blacks as a group appear to have been more motivated by the election than whites were. Yet whites in general, and Valentine supporters in particular, maintained their interest between the first primary and the run-off and voted at a reasonably high level.

Looking at the white vote in the district as a whole, after the first primary the Michaux staff placed their candidate's non-Durham white vote at less than 10 percent; that is, 90 percent or more of all whites in the eastern and Virginia-border coun-

> *In the five counties along the Virginia border . . . the second primary vote for Valentine was down 7.7 percent . . . [but] the Michaux vote increased an astonishing 22.2 percent.*

Table 5-4
Turnout in Virginia-Border Counties (2nd District, North Carolina)

County	First Primary Michaux	First Primary Valentine-Ramsey Total	First Primary Turnout as % of Regis.	Second Primary Michaux	Second Primary Valentine	Second Primary Turnout as % of Regis.
Caswell	2,355	3,205	52.0	2,879	3,128	56.4
Granville	3,439	5,124	62.3	4,029	4,983	64.8
Person	1,621	4,753	60.4	2,296	3,931	59.4
Vance	2,933	5,281	57.9	3,616	4,840	59.2
Warren	2,889	2,928	65.6	3,359	2,765	69.1
Total	13,237	21,291	59.3	16,179	19,647	60.6

ties were thought to have voted for a candidate other than Michaux. This estimate was probably not far off the mark.

Conclusion

As a project to mobilize black voters, the Michaux campaign was a major success. And given the political uncertainties that left even the composition of the 2nd district in doubt until 3-1/2 months before the election, its success was all the more remarkable.

The top members of the campaign staff remained together for about 10 days after the run-off, with Michaux and others working to find jobs for those who had played major roles in the campaign and holding debriefing sessions. Most staffers expressed surprise at the huge voter turnout. Had whites voted at their normal levels, the campaign effort among blacks would have assured Michaux a victory. Basically, however, the debriefing discussions were oriented more toward the future, including Michaux's own political future, than toward the past.

This writer believes that in its approach to black voters, the Michaux campaign made no serious tactical errors. Personal contact was the key to the effort and was tied in with a good program for using readily available registration records to identify potential voters. An able consultant with good data helped in the targeting of unregistered blacks. (But future campaigns cannot count upon access to drivers-license records.)

Of course, the campaign to reach blacks was not perfect. Everyone agreed on the value of phone banks and most people felt that television was useful, and both of those could have been used still more extensively if enough money had been available. Key staffers appeared to believe that "more of the same," rather than a whole new approach, might have made a difference.

Perhaps the major shortcoming of the Michaux campaign was its neglecting to foresee the magni-

After the first primary 90 percent or more of all whites in the eastern and Virginia-border counties were thought to have voted for a candidate other than Michaux.

tude of the white "backlash" at the polls (backlash in the sense that some whites viewed the mere presence of a black candidate as a threat). Yet the possibility (or probability) of such a backlash ought to have been particularly relevant to this campaign, given the majority-white population and whites' historical reluctance to support blacks in the typical southern political setting. Whatever the success of a drive to reach black voters, in the southern political equation the white factor demands special attention.

List of Persons Interviewed

James Andrews, field worker, North Carolina AFL-CIO (on leave with the Randolph Institute during the Michaux campaign)

Jesse Anglin, bank executive, Michaux campaign aide

Stanley Green, bank executive, Michaux campaign aide

Franklin Jones, independent businessman, Michaux campaign aide

Eric Michaux, brother and law partner of Mickey Michaux

Henry M. (Mickey) Michaux, congressional candidate

Kristen Petersen, communications director of the Michaux campaign

William Pulley, manager of the Valentine campaign

Christopher Scott, secretary-treasurer, North Carolina AFL-CIO

Kevin Smith, manager of the Michaux campaign (interviewed by telephone)

Dewitt Sullivan, treasurer of the Michaux campaign

133

Endnotes

1. Michael Barone, Grant Ujifusa, and Douglas Matthews, eds., *The Almanac of American Politics* (New York: E. P. Dutton, 1978), p. 629.

2. For Fountain's voting record, see various issues of the *Congressional Quarterly* or *The Almanac of American Politics* between 1973 and 1982. An interesting exception to Fountain's general conservatism was his attitude on regulating prescription drugs. As a member of the House Government Operations Committee, he frequently criticized the Food and Drug Administration (FDA) for laxity in allowing dangerous drugs to penetrate the market, and in the 1960s and 1970s, as chairman of the committee's subcommittee on Intergovernmental Relations and Human Resources, he held hearings at which he charged the FDA with operating behind a veil of secrecy.

3. *Congressional Quarterly,* 39 (October 10, 1981), 1959. Durham and Wake (Raleigh) counties were to be joined with Orange County (Chapel Hill) to constitute the new and largely urban 4th district. Chatham County was to be in Fountain's district, and Randolph County was to be in a more western district. Since Andrews already represented Durham and Wake counties and was well-known in Orange County, he seemed reasonably satisfied with the new arrangement.

4. Andrews was accustomed to Durham, since it had always been part of his district. Moreover, since Durham would be the proposed 4th district's Democratic bastion, it would presumably be useful to him in the general election. For Fountain, in contrast, Durham was hostile territory, and in any case he needed no Democratic cushion in the general election.

5. The date of the primary was still uncertain, however, because of problems with state legislative reapportionment, and would not be fixed until May 2. The primary had originally been scheduled for the first Tuesday in May, with the run-off to be held the first Tuesday in June. For a running account, see selected issues of the (Raleigh) *News and Observer* or the *Durham Morning Herald*.

6. The nine included the four eastern counties of Edgecombe, Halifax, Nash, and Wilson, and the five Virginia-border counties of Caswell, Granville, Person, Vance, and Warren. Caswell and Warren are rural and the other seven are mixed urban and rural. And to be certain of meeting population standards, the legislature also placed in the 2nd district a small township from Johnston County (most of Johnston County was in the eastern North Carolina 3rd district).

7. "Under the Dome," *News and Observer* (Raleigh, N.C.), April 1, 1982, sec. A, p. 12, and "Valentine Enters Race for New 2nd District Seat," *News and Observer*, April 16, 1982, sec. D, p. 1.

8. The usual turnout for each race in an off-year congressional election was about 32-35 percent of registered voters, but that figure is a bit deceptive because of the large institutional populations (universities, prisons, various homes) in the district. Usually students do not vote in university communities in North Carolina.

9. In North Carolina, many of the same rules apply both to partisan and nonpartisan organizations. But in matters of registration, there is a major difference between the two kinds of organization. A nonpartisan organization can contribute money to help a county board of elections sign up voters, whereas a political party or candidate cannot (see the example on page 115).

10. Franklin Jones asserted that the Hunt administration had encouraged black registration in Wilson County (Hunt's home county) in preparation for a 1984 bid against Republican Senator Jesse Helms. This was the case, he said, even though the white leaders of the Hunt organization in Wilson supported Valentine for the congressional seat.

11. Black registration in Durham would increase much more dramatically two years later, when Jesse Jackson was a factor in North Carolina's Democratic presidential primary and black attorney Ken Spaulding ran for Congress in the 2nd district's Democratic primary. (Spaulding lost to Valentine.)

135

12. At election time the percentage of blacks registered in Caswell County was slightly higher than the percentage of whites. In Warren County, the black registration percentage was within 1 point of the white. Warren County blacks had bitterly opposed the plan to locate a PCB toxic waste dump site in the county, calling the plan racist. This dispute apparently increased the political activism of the county's blacks.

13. People who supervised campaigns on the county level confirmed that educators played a significant role.

14. "2nd Congressional District, North Carolina, A Survey of Voter Attitudes and Opinions," prepared for Mickey Michaux by Cooper Associates, Inc., Batesville, Virginia, June 1983.

15. Warren is the only majority-black county in the district (60 percent). The other counties range from 50 percent black (Edgecombe) to 31 percent black (Person).

6. ORGANIZING AND EDUCATING FOR SUCCESSFUL MOBILIZATION

Thomas E. Cavanagh

Having scrutinized four campaigns to educate black voters, we can now begin to identify the factors associated with successful mobilization of the black vote. The criterion for "success" is straightforward: a measurable increase in the turnout rate of a targeted group.

Case studies have their limits, of course, especially when all the cases represent relatively "successful" outcomes. Inclusion of one or more "unsuccessful" cases would have enabled us to establish that a given variable is critical to organizational efforts because it is present in the successful cases and absent in the unsuccessful ones—or that the variable is detrimental because it is present in the unsuccessful cases and absent in the successful ones. Nonetheless, when a given factor is present in all four successful cases we can at least infer that it is important for mobilizing the black vote—or, at the very least, that it does not detract from such an effort.

Even if a mobilization effort itself is successful, the favored candidate may not be. Turnout gains among one group may be offset by turnout gains among supporters of a different candidate or party. In fact, one of the thorniest questions in the study of voter turnout is whether voter education efforts can really make a difference in election results. The classic Wolfinger and Rosenstone study, *Who Votes?*, found that universal turnout would cause only a marginal change in the composition of the national electorate in terms of its partisanship and attitudes.[1] This has frequently been interpreted to mean that fluctuations in turnout have no effect on elections and, by extension, that registration drives are a waste of effort. Yet such a conclusion is not

Clearly, under some circumstances the presence or absence of voter mobilization activity can mean the difference between the success or the failure of a given candidate.

necessarily implied by *Who Votes?*, especially if one is more concerned with local than with national elections, for contextual factors also play a role.

For example, Wolfinger and Rosenstone determined that in states with patronage systems, employees of the state government vote at unusually high levels in gubernatorial elections,[2] which suggests that political organization and the perception of a direct personal stake in the outcome of an election can stimulate voter participation. An impressive number of studies over the years have also shown that personal contact increases turnout.[3] Thus, even if the partisanship and attitudes of nonvoters are similar to those of voters, it does not necessarily follow that the nonvoters mobilized in a given campaign will be a *random* subset of the population of nonvoters. If organizational efforts are carefully—and differentially—targeted, some groups of voters with distinctive political allegiances can be mobilized more than others.

Under three conditions, a change in the turnout rate of a population group (e.g., blacks) can significantly alter the political composition of a local electorate, even while no change is perceptible in the composition of the national electorate. The three conditions are as follows:

- the target population group makes up a higher proportion of the local electorate than of the national electorate;
- the target population group is disproportionately loyal to a given party or candidate relative to the local electorate; and
- the target population group increases its voter turnout at a higher rate than does the rest of the local electorate.

Moreover, if another condition obtains—if the division of votes is so close that the target group's increased share of voters is greater than the winning candidate's eventual plurality—then by definition an increase in turnout can alter the *outcome* of an election.

All four conditions characterize the situation of blacks in many central cities throughout the country and in many counties in the rural South.

To actualize the potential of the black vote, then, blacks must first be made aware of their leverage over election outcomes.

- Blacks are at or near a majority of the voting-age population in many of those jurisdictions.
- Blacks are overwhelmingly Democratic and they overwhelmingly support black candidates against white candidates who are perceived as hostile to their interests.
- The rate of increase in black turnout between 1980 and 1984 was more than twice the national rate of increase.[4]
- In campaigns marked by racial polarization, small differences in black and white population percentages have resulted in close divisions of the vote.

Thus, it would be a mistake to generalize from national findings to particular local situations. Clearly, under some circumstances the presence or absence of voter mobilization activity can mean the difference between the success or the failure of a given candidate.

Certainly, the experience of Chicago should give pause to the skeptics. During Harold Washington's mayoral campaign, Chicago met all the conditions that can alter the composition of a local electorate: the black population makes up 40 percent of the local electorate; 99 percent of blacks cast their votes for Washington; and black voter turnout increased by a remarkable 30 percentage points. In addition, blacks and whites were severely polarized during the campaign: Washington's victory was just one manifestation of a revolt of Chicago's blacks against the long-standing domination of the city's Democratic party structure by white ethnic groups hostile to black interests in such domains as housing, education, and police protection.[5]

Another factor was present in Chicago, though, one that often marks successful black candidacies—the belief that a black could win. Washington himself stipulated that before he would enter the mayoral race, enough blacks had to be registered to put him within striking distance of a plurality in the Democratic mayoral primary. The perception of the *possibility* of victory was a key ingredient in the success of the Chicago voter education effort. Likewise, the perception of the possibility of victory was so essential to Michaux's campaign in North Caro-

A successful voter education effort is difficult to construct from scratch; a more promising approach is to build upon a social and political infrastructure already in place.

> *Close supervision and continual monitoring of the progress of registration have a strong bearing on the success of the enterprise.*

lina that his staff distributed detailed analyses of district voting patterns to persuade blacks that a black could be elected to Congress.

This element was widely noted by the participants in a conference on "Race and Political Strategy" held by the Joint Center for Political Studies in 1983. Democratic National Committee Vice Chairman Tony Harrison noted that "the more blacks believe that a black candidate can win, the greater the turnout is."[6] Veteran Baltimore political consultant Larry Gibson agreed that "one problem in getting massive turnouts for black candidates is the [lack of] belief that the candidate can win. That sense of momentum, that sense of its being possible, is so important that if you had to choose between that and converting the opposition, my preference would be to educate your people that it can be done."[7]

An interesting corollary to this point was developed in the course of Jesse Jackson's campaign for the 1984 Democratic presidential nomination: victory can be defined in ways other than winning an election. Since Jackson's chances of attaining the nomination were slim, he defined "victory" in terms of other campaign objectives: increasing black registration, encouraging the candidacy of black candidates for local office, and articulating a progressive agenda to augment the political influence of blacks and other disadvantaged groups within the Democratic party.[8] By redefining "victory" in terms of achievable objectives, Jackson developed a highly innovative strategy that might prove useful in future efforts to mobilize black voters.

To actualize the potential of the black vote, then, blacks must first be made aware of their leverage over election outcomes. This awareness is what leads black voters to turn out. To create this awareness and bring the voters out, groups and individuals need both an organizational framework and techniques of educating voters.

Organizational Framework

All four of the voter education efforts discussed in this volume built upon existing networks of black political activists who had a long history of close collaboration in electoral and lobbying campaigns. A successful voter education effort is difficult to construct from scratch; a more promising approach is to build upon a social and political infrastructure already in place.

The groups active in the Chicago registration campaign had worked together on a variety of projects for a decade; and POWER, which took the lead in voter registration efforts in that city, was an outgrowth of a previous campaign to protest cutbacks in state spending on public assistance. The Wilson Goode campaign in Philadelphia grew out of activities that linked blacks and white liberals during several years: it built upon the experiences gained in the 1978 charter referendum fight and in Charles Bowser's 1979 mayoral campaign. In both Birmingham and North Carolina, the A. Philip Randolph Institute played an essential role in voter mobilization activities. And perhaps the most interesting instance of the phenomenon of a political infrastructure's developing over time was the evolution of Birmingham's neighborhood planning associations, which began as vehicles for coordinating local antipoverty efforts and became major forces for black electoral advancement.

Since black voter education campaigns are coalition efforts, the allocation of tasks among the various groups involved requires considerable care—to avoid running afoul of legal restrictions or creating internecine rivalries. The clearest division of functional responsibilities occurred in Chicago, where the most conspicuous success was recorded. POWER conducted outreach registration of people on public assistance; CBUC concentrated on voter education; and VOTE Community assumed responsibility for the media campaign.

Interestingly, all three groups—POWER, CBUC, and VOTE Community—were active in registration and education activity before each election as well as in get-out-the-vote activity on the day of the election. Involving the same groups in both registration and GOTV activity appears to be a way of surmounting one of the major problems encountered in the past by black voter education programs, namely,

Support from the local government and local candidates is another important ingredient in a successful registration program.

the failure to turn out many newly registered voters because registration and GOTV are undertaken by different organizations.[9] Each of the four campaigns improvised a locally relevant solution to the generally encountered problem of trying to coordinate the voter education and GOTV phases of the mobilization campaign.

In Philadelphia, the fact that the bulk of the mobilization efforts was conducted by the candidates' organizations had the effect of unifying registration and GOTV under the same roof. In addition, a considerable core of community volunteers shifted from nonpartisan voter education activities to partisan GOTV work for the Goode campaign. Thus, the same individuals were involved in both phases of the mobilization effort, even though they conducted each phase under different auspices.

But in our other two communities, the overlap between registration and GOTV activities was less systematic. In Birmingham, the NAACP was involved in both activities, but neighborhood planning associations, churches, and the League of Women Voters specialized in the seemingly "nonpartisan" registration effort, whereas much of the ostensibly more "partisan" GOTV work was handled by labor unions and candidate organizations. A similar pattern was seen in North Carolina: churches and tenant organizations were more important in the registration campaign, whereas labor unions, black county-level political action groups, and the League of Conservation Voters were active in GOTV activities. Michaux's campaign workers were active in both phases, but the overall disjunction between voter education and GOTV may have detracted somewhat from the ultimate success of the effort.

If large sums of money can be raised, the Chicago experience suggests that the expense of a saturation media campaign can probably be justified.

Close supervision and continual monitoring of the progress of registration have a strong bearing on the success of the enterprise. The Goode workers in Philadelphia were given explicit targets to meet in each electoral division, and the campaign's headquarters kept a close, ongoing watch on whether these targets were met. A study of a black voter education drive in Detroit sheds some light on this matter. The study found that the degree of supervision had a lot to do with the different increases in registration in different parts of the city. The local Democratic organization in Detroit was more proficient at giving directions to grassroots workers than were the various nonpartisan groups involved in registration, which suggests that exclusive reliance on nonpartisan groups may not be an optimum strategy.[10]

Support from the local government and local candidates is another important ingredient in a successful registration program. In Birmingham, Mayor Richard Arrington and Deputy Registrar Ornie McAlpin clearly were major contributors to the success of registration activities. In North Carolina, the state government was responsive to the political needs of Governor James Hunt, whose senatorial aspirations were deemed likely to benefit from increased black registration. In Philadelphia, the support of Mayor William Green and of the chief registration commissioner were positive factors. In all three locations, the activities of black candidates running for county and municipal office spurred registration and turnout. The situation in Chicago was more problematic. A court case was necessary before on-site registration at public assistance offices could take place. Although ultimately local election officials did not stand in the way of the effort, on-site registration would have been hard to implement if there had not been favorable judicial intervention.

To the extent that any financial information could be gathered, it appears that an extensive media campaign of the type seen in Chicago is very expensive (costing well into six figures) but also very effective. In the other three locations, outlays were relatively modest—$50,000 or less for voter registration and GOTV—and much more reliance was placed on labor-intensive activities (such as canvassing and mobile registration) by volunteers. If large sums of money can be raised, the Chicago experience suggests that the expense of a saturation media campaign can probably be justified.

> *Procedural flexibility and ease of registration contributed to the success of all four registration campaigns.*

Techniques of Educating Voters

Not surprisingly, procedural flexibility and ease of registration contributed to the success of all four

> *The tradition of door-to-door canvassing appears to be giving way to other techniques of outreach to target populations of black nonvoters.*

registration campaigns. Some of the registration procedures employed were quite innovative, such as mail-in registration in Philadelphia, "roving registrars" in North Carolina, and librarians serving as deputy registrars in Birmingham. And the importance of the on-site registration programs in Chicago cannot be overestimated: according to the figures of the Chicago Board of Elections, fully 77,000 people were registered at public aid and unemployment offices. It is a well-established finding in the political science literature that the more convenient the registration system, the more likely individuals are to register.[11] This principle is fully consonant with the findings of the four case studies.

The tradition of door-to-door canvassing appears to be giving way to other techniques of outreach to target populations of black nonvoters. Clearly, registering people who are gathered together in a group is more efficient than registering people who are approached individually. If the objective is to register the most people for the least expenditure of effort, then it is most useful to sponsor high-visibility activities reaching out to large numbers of people gathered in a single location. In Philadelphia, a preference emerged for stationing registrars at shopping centers and other walk-in locations with large numbers of black patrons, as opposed to engaging in tedious door-to-door canvassing. A feature of several of the four voter education efforts was registration at rallies, church and tenant meetings, and schools. In general, it appears to make the most sense, from the perspective of both the registrant and the registrar, to bring the registrar to a site where large numbers of potential registrants are likely to be congregating for nonpolitical reasons.

Of course, an extensive media campaign of the type employed in Chicago can also dramatically increase the visibility of the registration effort. Political organizer Larry Gibson articulated the rationale for media campaigning in discussing Baltimore's 1982 voter education campaign:

> I find . . . over the years as I run additional campaigns . . . that I move more and more *away* from grass-roots organization as something that is

cost-effective, useful, and even achievable. . . . By far the most powerful tool with which to communicate to people is television. There simply is no competitor. You buy, and in one second, you go up every alley, into every street, every block, into every house.[12]

In the four local environments studied, the political loyalties of blacks were sufficiently uniform and predictable that the four voter education efforts could simply concentrate on locating unregistered blacks and then target their efforts accordingly. This was usually done by comparing census tract and block data to ward and precinct data and comparing the number of registered blacks to the black voting-age population for a given geographical unit. Occasionally more esoteric tools were utilized, such as city directories in Birmingham or the fortuitously available computer tape of drivers' licenses in North Carolina.

In some cases, an effort was made to identify and locate more specific subgroups of the black population. For example, in Chicago a great emphasis was placed on registering younger blacks, because of their traditionally low participation rate; that was one reason for the emphasis on black soul-music radio stations. The Michaux campaign was especially concerned with signing up older blacks, who were often reluctant to vote because of the history of intimidation of black voters in the South. (It is helpful to associate each target group with an organizational infrastructure, such as schools for reaching the young or senior citizen centers for the elderly.)

To be effective, the messages conveyed as part of a voter education campaign should be kept simple and direct. The two most noteworthy Chicago slogans, "We shall see in '83" and "Come alive on October Five," conveyed a sense of excitement, set a date for action, and helped contribute to the pervasive atmosphere of a crusade. In the South, reminding blacks of the history behind the Voting Rights Act can invest registration with emotional significance. The leaflets distributed in North Carolina bearing pictures of Martin Luther King, Jr., and other heroes with the caption "They died for you"

To be effective, the messages conveyed as part of a voter education campaign should be kept simple and direct.

played effectively on this potential, as did the slogan "A right you don't use is a right you can lose." In Philadelphia, given how much blacks disliked Frank Rizzo and admired his opponent, Wilson Goode, it was sufficient to point out that "You can't vote for Wilson Goode unless you are registered." The common thread running through all these messages is the notion of removing the act of registering to vote from the context of "politics as usual" and making the candidates and issues at stake appear vitally important to black interests. Abstract appeals are unlikely to make many inroads into generations-old disaffection. Concrete and locally relevant messages are essential.

Further research of the type presented in this study would answer additional questions that could not be addressed here. For one example, how readily can one generalize from these four cases to black voter education efforts in support of white candidates? For another example, people involved in black voter education activity have frequently stressed the need for studies of how to motivate lower-income blacks, whose interest in politics and whose relationship to the wider social and economic structure are often marginal, at best. Case studies examining such issues could make valuable contributions to both analysts and practitioners concerned with voter participation.

Abstract appeals are unlikely to make many inroads into generations-old disaffection. Concrete and locally relevant messages are essential.

Mobilizing the black vote requires strategies and techniques designed specifically to reflect blacks' historically ambivalent relationship to America's political process. Although government has sometimes taken initiatives to ameliorate the condition of blacks, blacks have generally been kept on the receiving end of power for some 200 years. But as these four case studies indicate, a variety of approaches to targeting the black population for voter education activity can bear fruit. The black vote is often termed a "sleeping giant." With hard work and imagination, the sleeping giant can be awakened.

Endnotes

1. Raymond E. Wolfinger and Steven J. Rosenstone, *Who Votes?* (New Haven: Yale University Press, 1980).

2. Ibid.; Bernard R. Berelson, Paul F. Lazarsfeld, and William N. McPhee, *Voting* (Chicago: University of Chicago Press, 1954); Samuel J. Eldersveld, "Experimental Propaganda Techniques and Voting Behavior," *American Political Science Review*, 50 (March 1956), 154-165; Gerald H. Kramer, "The Effects of Precinct-Level Canvassing on Voter Behavior," *Public Opinion Quarterly*, 34 (Winter 1970-1971), 560-572; Raymond E. Wolfinger, "The Influence of Precinct Work on Voting Behavior," *Public Opinion Quarterly*, 27 (Fall 1963), 387-398.

3. These findings are summarized in Thomas E. Cavanagh, *Black Voter Participation in the United States: A Review of the Literature* (Washington, D.C.: Joint Center for Political Studies, 1983).

4. Thomas E. Cavanagh, *Inside Black America*, (Washington, D.C.: Joint Center for Political Studies, 1985), p. 12.

5. For an excellent analysis relating city governance to black mobilization in Chicago, see Paul Kleppner, *Chicago Divided: The Making of a Black Mayor* (DeKalb, Ill.: Northern Illinois University Press, 1985). The recent history of black electoral participation in Chicago is extensively discussed in Michael B. Preston, "The Resurgence of Black Voting in Chicago, 1955-1983," in *The Making of the Mayor: Chicago, 1983*, eds. Melvin G. Holli and Paul M. Green (Grand Rapids, Mich.: William B. Eerdmans, 1984).

6. *Race and Political Strategy*, ed. Thomas E. Cavanagh (Washington, D.C.: Joint Center for Political Studies, 1983), p. 34.

7. Ibid., p. 36.

8. Thomas E. Cavanagh and Lorn S. Foster, *Jesse Jackson's Campaign: The Primaries and Cau-*

cuses (Washington, D.C.: Joint Center for Political Studies, 1984).

9. Charles V. Hamilton, "Voter Registration Drives and Turnout: A Report on the Harlem Electorate," *Political Science Quarterly,* 92 (Spring 1977), 43-46.

10. Paul Carton, *Mobilizing the Black Community: The Effects of Personal Contact Campaigning on Black Voter Behavior* (Washington, D.C.: Joint Center for Political Studies, 1984).

11. Wolfinger and Rosenstone, chapter 4. Curiously, however, Wolfinger and Rosenstone also found that "with other variables controlled, people in states that authorize deputy registrars are no likelier to vote" (p. 76).

12. *Race and Political Strategy,* pp. 47-48.

JOINT CENTER FOR POLITICAL STUDIES BOARD OF GOVERNORS

Chairman
Wendell G. Freeland, Esq.
Freeland & Krontz
Pittsburgh, Pennsylvania

Vice Chairman
William B. Boyd
President
The Johnson Foundation
Racine, Wisconsin

Treasurer
Louis F. Martin
Assistant Vice President
  for Communications
Howard University
Washington, D.C.

Bishop John Hurst Adams
Chairman
Congress of National
  Black Churches
Washington, D.C.

Robert McCormick Adams
Secretary
Smithsonian Institution
Washington, D.C.

Lucius J. Barker
Edna F. Gellhorn University
  Professor of Public Affairs
  and Professor of Political
  Science
Washington University
St. Louis, Missouri

Charles U. Daly
Director
The Joyce Foundation
  and the Ireland Fund
Chicago, Illinois

Hortense Williams Dixon
Houston, Texas

The Hon. Mervyn Dymally
U.S. Representative
Washington, D.C.

Marian Wright Edelman
President
Children's Defense Fund
Washington, D.C.

Luther Hilton Foster
Chairman
Foster Associates, Inc.
Washington, D.C.

Jayne Brumley Ikard
Washington, D.C.

Robert C. Maynard
Editor, Publisher and President
Oakland Tribune
Oakland, California

Bernard Rapoport
Chairman
American Income Life
  Insurance Co.
Waco, Texas

Eddie N. Williams
President
Joint Center for Political Studies
Washington, D.C.

James D. Wolfensohn
James D. Wolfensohn, Inc.
New York, New York

Secretary to the Board
Eleanor Farrar
Vice President
Joint Center for Political Studies
Washington, D.C.

SELECTED JCPS PUBLICATIONS

Black Elected Officials: A National Roster, 1986, 15th edition. ISSN 0882-1593. $29.50.

Black Employment in City Government, 1973-1980, Peter Eisinger, 1983. ISBN 0-941410-32-3. $4.95

Blacks on the Move: A Decade of Demographic Change, William P. O'Hare, Jane-yu Li, Roy Chatterjee, and Margaret Shukur, abridged by Phillip Sawicki, 1982. ISBN 0-941410-25-0. $4.95.

The Changing Patterns of Black Family Income, 1960-1982, Henry E. Felder, 1984. ISBN 0-941410-43-9. $4.95.

Elected and Appointed Black Judges in the United States, 1986. ISSN 0889-3179. $10.00.

Focus, JCPS monthly newsletter. ISSN 0740-0195. $15.00 per annum.

Foreign Trade Policy and Black Economic Advancement: Proceedings of a JCPS Roundtable, 1981. ISBN 0-941410-19-6. $4.95.

How to Use Section 5 of the Voting Rights Act, third edition, Barbara Y. Phillips, 1984. ISBN 0-941410-27-7. $4.95.

Inside Black America: The Message of the Black Vote in the 1984 Elections, Thomas E. Cavanagh, 1986. ISBN 0-941410-47-1. $4.95.

The JCPS Congressional District Fact Book (1986 edition), compiled by JCPS staff, 1986. ISSN 0888-8957. $6.95.

Minorities and the Labor Market: Twenty Years of Misguided Policy, Richard McGahey and John Jeffries, 1985. ISBN 0-941410-53-6. $5.95.

Minority Vote Dilution, edited by Chandler Davidson, 1984. Available from Howard University Press, 2900 Van Ness St., Washington, DC 20008. $24.95.

Mobilizing the Black Community: The Effects of Personal Contact Campaigning on Black Voters, Paul Carton, 1984. ISBN 0-941410-42-0. $4.95.

The Nineteen Eighties: Prologue and Prospect, Kenneth B. Clark and John Hope Franklin, 1981. ISBN 0-941410-20-X. $2.95.

A Policy Framework for Racial Justice (statement by 30 black scholars), 1983. Introduction by Kenneth B. Clark and John Hope Franklin. ISBN 0-941410-30-7. $4.95.

A Policy Framework for Racial Justice (II): Black Initiative and Governmental Responsibility, 1987. Introduction by John Hope Franklin and Eleanor Holmes Norton. ISBN 0-941410-61-7. $6.95.

Public School Desegregation in the United States, 1968-1980, Gary Orfield, 1983. ISBN 0-941410-29-3. $4.95.

Race and Political Strategy, edited by Thomas E. Cavanagh, 1983. ISBN 0-941410-33-1. $4.95.

Thirty Years after Brown, Jennifer L. Hochschild, 1985. ISBN 0-941410-49-8. $4.95.

Trends, Prospects, and Strategies for Black Economic Progress, Andrew Brimmer, 1985. ISBN 0-941410-56-0. $5.95.

Wealth and Economic Status: A Perspective on Racial Inequity, William P. O'Hare, 1983. ISBN 0-941410-35-8. $4.95.

NOTES

NOTES

NOTES

NOTES

NOTES

NOTES